MOSAICS IN ROMAN BRITAIN

ANTHONY BEESON

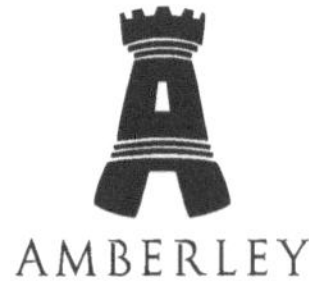

AMBERLEY

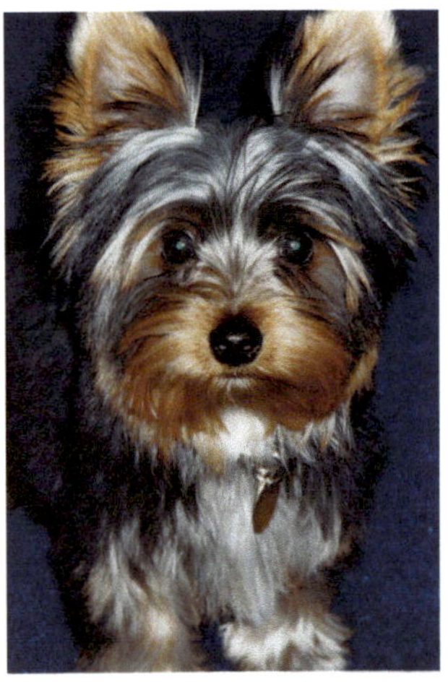

To the shade of Jasper O'Neill Beeson,
25.10.2003–5.12.2019,
who loved unconditionally.

First published 2022

Amberley Publishing
The Hill, Stroud,
Gloucestershire, GL5 4EP

www.amberley-books.com

ISBN: 978 1 4456 8988 3 (print)
ISBN: 978 1 4456 8989 0 (ebook)

British Library Cataloguing in Publication Data.
A catalogue record for this book is available from the British Library.

Typeset in 10pt on 13pt Celeste.
Typesetting by SJmagic DESIGN SERVICES, India.

Appointed GPSR EU Representative: Easy Access System Europe Oü, 16879218
Address: Mustamäe tee 50, 10621, Tallinn, Estonia
Contact Details: gpsr.requests@easproject.com, +358 40 500 3575

Contents

Introduction

Of all the arts of Roman Britain, mosaic pavements have left the most obvious traces and captured the public's imagination. Nearly two thousand are recorded from Cornwall to Scotland, although only a handful survive or are publicly displayed. Britain was 'officially' part of the Roman Empire for some 367 years – the same length of time separating us from Cromwell's Protectorate. Romano-British culture did not cease in AD 410 when a political decision severed the province from Rome, and everyday life continued and adapted over the following centuries. At Hucclecote, Gloucestershire, pavements were laid after AD 395 and in 2020, radiocarbon dating of charcoal and bone from below a wall at Chedworth suggests that Room 28's mosaic was laid after AD 424. Excavation illustrates that in this era of transition, many mosaics were carefully patched or fitted with tile or flagstones.

During those centuries when she was part of the empire, Britain developed her own form of *Romanitas* or Roman-styled culture. Allied in some ways to those of other northern provinces, the mosaic tradition of Britannia is otherwise insular, often displaying singularity both in design and choice of subject. Geometric mosaics appear to have been most favoured

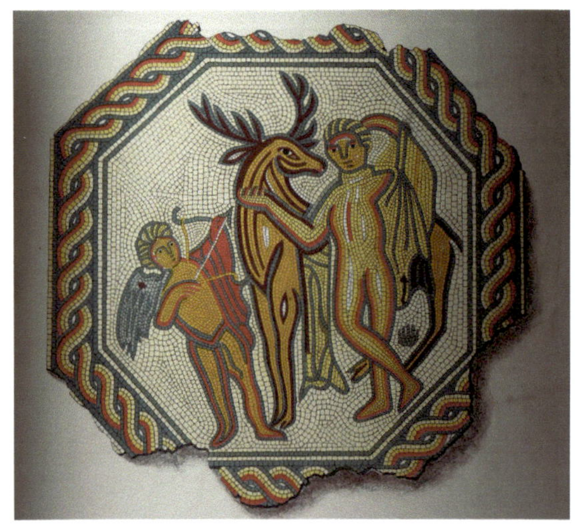

A very rare subject from Highcross Street, Leicester, taken from Ovid's *Metamorphoses*. Apollo's favourite, Cyparissus, and his beloved stag whom he unwittingly killed. Cupid shoots an arrow of love. Lithograph by H. Ecroyd Smith, 1850. (Author's collection)

in the province, possibly through a native love of pattern, but plenty of figurative subjects also survive. Lacking the intense skill found in the art of mosaic in some parts of the Roman world British mosaicists still achieved originality in design and produced pavements that were the equal to those of other provinces. The 2019 excavation of Boxford's Triumphs of Pelops and Bellerophon mosaic, with its subtly interlinked mythological subjects, mostly unknown elsewhere, and whose main Pelops composition survives only on a Syrian mosaic and another in Spain, provides a light into the cultural world of the elite of late Roman Britain. Likewise the mosaic of the tragic love of Dido and Æneas from Low Ham, Somerset, taken from Virgil's *Æneid*, is unmatched anywhere else in the Roman Empire and again indicates the literary culture of the Romano-British upper classes. It is notable that, unlike many provinces, Britannia's figurative mosaics show little interest in the arena's bloodshed or in portraying genre topics beyond hunting. They mostly depict scenes from literature or Graeco-Roman mythology. These are often condensed to a couple of figures within a panel and taken from well-known compositions, such as Achilles on Skyros, or drawn from the myths recounted in literary sources such as Ovid's *Metamorphoses* or Hyginus' *Fabulae*. Nevertheless, it would have been expected that the viewer would have sufficient *paideia* (culture) to recognise these artistic aide memoires and, where necessary, link them mentally to understand the choice of subject and have total comprehension of whatever message was being visually or mentally portrayed. A knowledge of the iconography of deities and heroes, so vital for the art historian to identify who is portrayed in classical art, must have been commonplace. The outmoded belief that somehow Roman Britain was devoid of culture is further belied by the writings of two of its native theologians: Patricius (St Patrick) and Pelagius. The latter with his doctrine of free will and denial of original sin proved so popular with many in the province and so rattled the Roman Christian establishment that Germanus was sent to Britain to combat Pelagianism in or around AD 429.

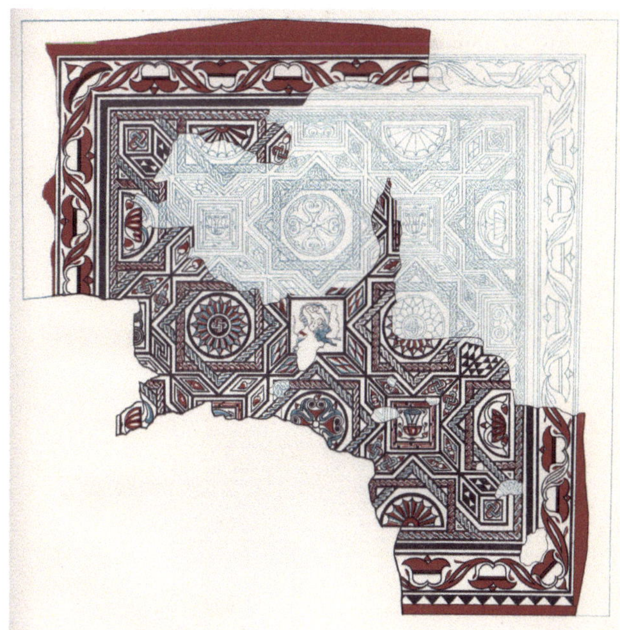

The huge mosaic from Old Broad Street, London, featuring either Europa or Bacchus was found in 1854 and taken to the Crystal Palace but never displayed and is now lost. (Author's collection)

The modern study of Romano-British mosaics owes much to the enthusiasm of Dr David Smith (1924–2016) who, in 1952, compiled a corpus of Romano-British mosaics as an appendix to his doctoral thesis and amassed a photographic archive at Newcastle University. Thereafter, apart from the Fishbourne excavations and Anne Rainey's *Mosaics in Roman Britain* (1973), mosaics studies in Britain remained dormant until 1979 and the founding, by Smith and other academic enthusiasts, of The Association for the Study and Preservation of Roman Mosaics (ASPROM). This resulted in an explosion of interest and research in Britain. ASPROM was a British branch of AIEMA (L'Association International pour l'Étude de la Mosaïque Antique), which had been founded to foster international mosaic studies and encourage each member country to produce a corpus of all Roman mosaics discovered within its borders. ASPROM's foundation coincided with the interest in mosaics engendered by the excavation of the Orpheus mosaic at Littlecote in Wiltshire. Its strength was that it welcomed members from all walks of life and levels of interest and its membership was not purely university or museum based. Papers by its members have continued to be published in its annual bulletin *Mosaic* that now forms a chronicle of British mosaic research. A complete file of *Mosaic* is available to the public on prior application in the art periodicals collection at Bristol Reference Library. On Smith's retirement, his slide archive was sorted by the author (then ASPROM's and the Roman Research Trust's archivist) before being presented with his books to the Institute of Classical Studies in London. Smith identified the work of several mosaicists that he based on particular urban centres, naming them the Corinian, Durnovarian, Petuarian and Durobrivan schools, which, although a useful classification, perhaps aggrandised what must have been just a collection of small family firms. This quartet was later expanded by Peter Johnson.

The 'Bible' of the mosaic researcher is the great work compiled between 2002 and 2010 by David Neal and Stephen Cosh entitled *Roman Mosaics of Britain*. Within its four volumes (and forthcoming appendix) every recorded mosaic discovered in Britain is listed. Research in previous centuries was the domain of the gentleman antiquary. John Aubrey, Sir Richard Colt Hoare, Samuel Lysons, Charles Roach Smith, William Bathurst and Thomas Morgan are just a few of many to whom the modern world owes a debt for recording mosaic discoveries. Alas, most early discoveries did not survive. Public authorities had no interest in their preservation and, unless the landowner took steps to safeguard them, they soon were lost to frost, rain or visitors. The 'curiosity of rustics' saw the destruction of many newly discovered mosaics. Samuel Hasell's 1827 discoveries at Littledean, Somerset, were destroyed by country folk for souvenirs and charms before he could record them and at Wroxeter, Shropshire, another was 'torn to pieces' in a day by visitors from Shrewsbury. As late as the 1990s a mosaic at Widford church and a tessellated pavement at Worsham, Oxfordshire, had to be reburied to foil souvenir hunters. The villa at Carisbrooke on the Isle of Wight presented mosaics and intact painted wall plaster when excavated in 1859. The vicar's refusal to allow a cover building to be erected to protect the remains saw the loss of, first, the plaster and then the mosaic. A year later the island's antiquarian Dr Ernest Wilkins memorably commented 'The Genius of Destruction is swift and sure'.

Even if sheltered within a building, unless that was maintained, survival was precarious and more often than not floors were lost. Mosaics sent to country houses and institutions for protection even as late as the 1950s were lucky to survive. Those from Pit Meads once at Longleat have vanished. An impressive mosaic from Old Broad Street, London, with a

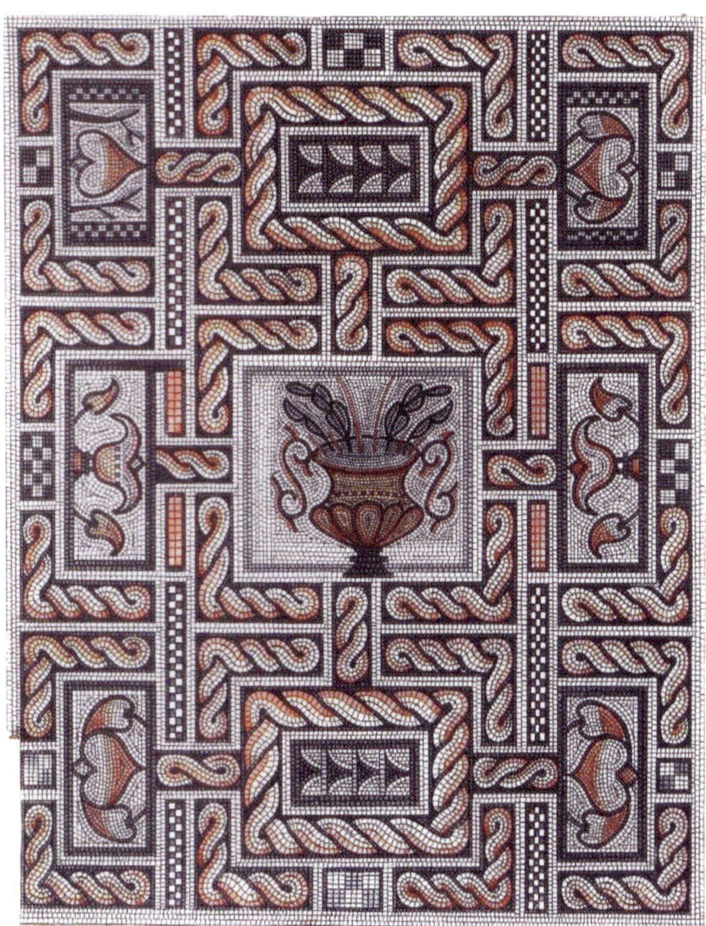

The doomed
Carisbrooke mosaic
engraved by George
Hillier in 1859.
(Author's collection)

damaged central panel depicting either Bacchus on a leopard or the Rape of Europa was sent to the Crystal Palace for safekeeping in 1854. Never displayed, it was presumably stored in the basement and destroyed or buried in the 1936 conflagration. Newton St Loe's mosaics, found during the construction of the Great Western Railway, were carefully lifted by Brunel and first displayed at Keynsham railway station. They were then sent to Bristol's early museum as a more appropriate guardian but now survive as hundreds of fragments.

For those mosaics that find sanctuary in a museum the likelihood is that they will never be fully displayed to the public. Far worse is to read the note 'discarded' in a museum's records when trying to locate one. A mosaic from Caerwent in Newport Museum ended up as road ballast through corporation philistinism in the 1920s. Unlike Germany, Britain lacks many museums devoted to Roman art or designed to accommodate mosaics, which by their nature take up floor or wall space. What is needed is a national Romano-British art collection or at least regional museums devoted to the subject in the manner of the regional Tate Galleries. Many museums have historically found mosaics a nuisance to accommodate, not recognising their importance as early British artworks. As a result museum stores throughout the country are full of mosaic panels or floors never seen by the public together with much Roman stonework excavated only to be buried again. Bristol Museum, for example, still kindly stores two rolled mosaics excavated in Cirencester in the 1960s that have never returned home, as well as its own mosaic panels from Brislington, West Dean and Newton St Loe. Even the British Museum controversially removed the important Hinton St Mary mosaic from display to join others such as the Withington Orpheus panels in storage and now only exhibits the central roundel possibly depicting Christ. An action rather akin to the National Gallery cutting a detail out from a Van Dyke painting in order to save wall space.

This volume is intended as a popular introduction to Romano-British mosaics, their construction, mythology and imagery. Emphasis is given to subjects that were singularly popular in the province and notes imagery that is unique to Britain. It includes a discussion on the newly discovered Boxford mosaic and what it discloses about classical culture among Britannia's upper classes.

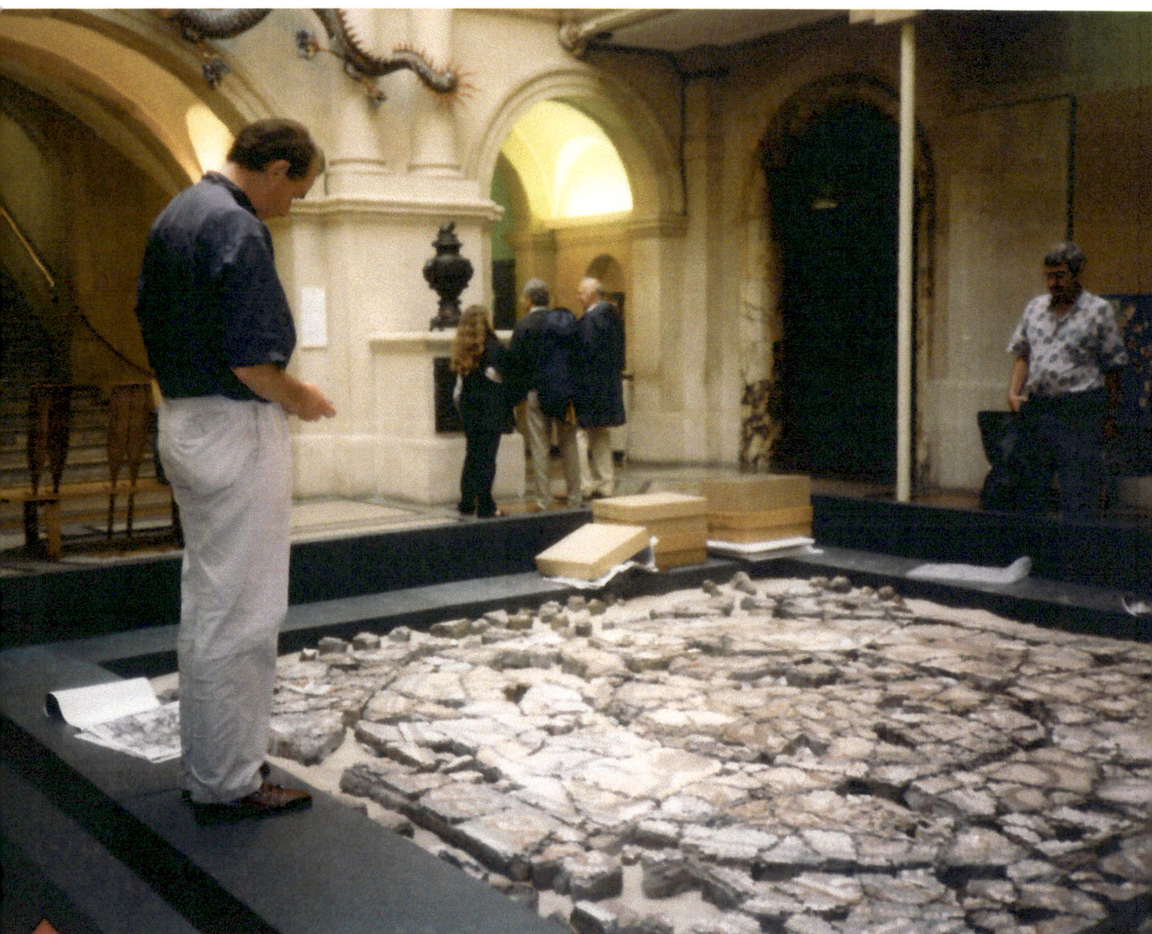

The author identifying and reassembling the hundreds of fragments of the Newton St Loe Orpheus mosaic in Bristol Museum. Now in storage in panels. July 2000. (Georgie Webb)

1

The Origins of Opus Tessellatum

Clay and plaster floors inset with pebbles, sometimes forming simple patterns, have been found in Bronze Age Crete and Mycenaean Greece, but the 2018 excavation of a large Bronze Age Hittite building at Uşaklı Höyük, Turkey, uncovered the earliest known example of what equates to a true mosaic floor. This 3 m x 7 m mosaic of black, white and light red triangles in black bordered panels, formed of irregular stones, raises new questions concerning the origin of mosaic flooring in Bronze Age Near Eastern public architecture. That the craft survived is proven by finds at Gordian where there are examples of mosaic floored houses from the eighth century BC and later.

Likewise the idea of decorating plain plaster or clay floors with beach or river pebbles also lingered in Greece. Plain unpatterned floors, sometimes employing mixed coloured pebbles, have been found in seventh-century Greek religious sanctuaries. Patterned mosaics first appear in late fifth-century Greece. By the time that the new town of Olynthos was founded in 432 BC the art form had made considerable progress and mosaics included figured work. Olynthos was destroyed in 348 BC but by the late fourth century some of the most beautiful figural pebble mosaics to survive from antiquity were being laid at Pella. Lead strips were by now used to emphasise features such as profiles and curls.

Mosaics of cut tesserae apparently originated in Greece and Sicily during the third century BC and the claimants for the earliest known tessellated mosaics, from around 260–50 BC, partially survive at the House of Ganymede at Morgantina. Their sophistication shows that they were not the first of their kind, but what is notable at this stage is the coexistence and sometimes incorporation of both pebbles and cut tesserae on the same pavement. This coexistence also occurs in Alexandria where mosaics were being regularly laid by the third century BC. Here, as in many Hellenistic kingdoms, the mosaic art was nurtured and, by the first half of the second century BC, mosaicists using miniscule tesserae and a wide palette of colours could produce mosaic copies of paintings that aped the originals. This exceptional technique is known as *opus vermiculatum* and picture panels known as *emblemata* that were made in the studio and set into terracotta or stone frames measuring up to 1 metre square were highly prized among the later Roman aristocracy and set into the centre of floors as illustrations of wealth. They could of course be removed and sold should the need arise. Greater wealth could provide a whole mosaic in the technique such as the fabulous 5.82 m x 3.13 m copy of a Hellenistic painting (probably by Apelles) of Alexander at the battle of the Issos from Pompeii's House of the Faun.

Rome saw and desired mosaics and other forms of decorative flooring in Hellenistic Greece, Egypt, Punic North Africa and Sicily and adopted them. Britain would start to get her own mosaics within a decade of her conquest in AD 43.

Romans called decorative mosaic work *opus tessellatum*. Mosaicists may well have been connected to architects and building firms. The unique inscription on a mosaic from Lucus (St Paul-les-Romans), France, reads 'Quintus Amiteius architect' rather than 'mosaicist'. Unfortunately there is no certain signature on a British mosaic to tell us who laid it, although the odd device is sometimes seen as the mark of an illiterate and the letters 'TER' on a mosaic at Bignor has led some to invent Terentius. The latter, however, may equally relate to the lost figure within the panel it accompanies such as the Muse Terpsichore. Throughout antiquity more than seventy signatures on mosaics remain. Some state *ex officina* ('from the workshop of...'), suggesting that several mosaicists were employed on commissions. The craft was considered inferior to that of the mural painter as the AD 301 Edict of Diocletian proves. There the *musaearius* receives sixty denarii a day and the *tessellarius* received fifty (both with 'maintenance' [board]), which equalled the pay of marine shipwrights and blacksmiths respectively. Wall painters received seventy denarii and figure painters received 150. The *musaearius* was probably either a wall mosaicist or skilled at figurative and decorative mosaics, whereas the *tessellarius* made plain tessellated or simple geometric pavements. The AD 337 Constantinian edict shows that mosaicists worked in fairly small family firms as it exempted them from public service so they could concentrate entirely on their artform and train their sons.

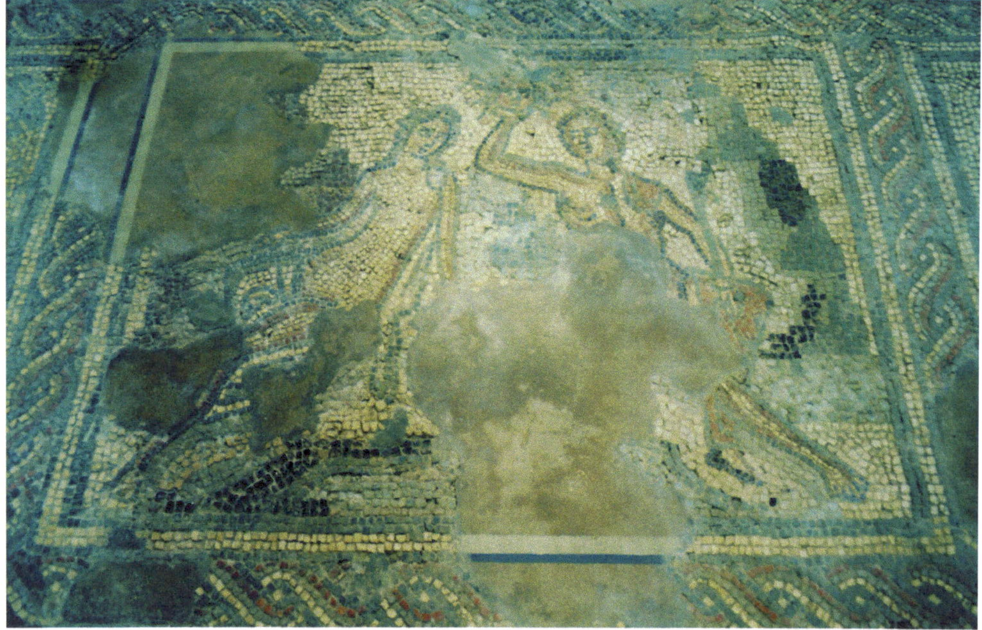

Brading's elegant rendition of Perseus showing Andromeda the reflected head of the Gorgon Medusa in a rock pool. A popular composition in Pompeian mural painting, but seemingly unique in mosaic. Perseus holds the hooked harpe-sword, the gift of his father Jupiter (Zeus). (Author's photograph)

2

Laying Mosaics

The Roman writer Vitruvius gave firm instructions on founding a floor but not on laying mosaics. Early British mosaics are well founded and often firmly bedded in *opus signinum*. Standards deteriorated after the second century often with shallow bedding mortar and no sub-base. Boxford's mosaic was only laid on a compacted 3 cm bed of sand over a pounded chalk and clay base. Evidence there suggests that its coarse border was completed before the mosaic perhaps to form a working surface. Sub-bedding mortar might be scoured, painted or strings used to give basic guidlines for layout. Fine lime mortar provided the final base and tesserae would be tapped level into it with a wooden block. Perhaps a square metre of mosaic might be laid in a day and when completed the mosaic would be grouted. Time would be needed for drying out. It is likely that mosaicists worked as part of a builder-decorators team as the final polishing could not be done until the mess of plastering and painting ceiling and walls was past. Plaster is believed to have adhered easier to ceramic tesserae, hence their presence in a narrow strip surrounding some stone borders. After a mortar quarter-skirting had been applied, the mosaic's surface was cleaned and ground to a polish with silver sand, water and grinding stones. A quartzite grinder was found at Littlecote. Grinding with sand and water enhances the colour of stones negating the use of oils or wax.

Sourcing Materials

Recent research into the origins of tesserae used in mosaics suggest the existence of a sophisticated supply chain with materials transported hundreds of miles throughout Britain. In the south the quarries around Kimmeridge Bay produced tesserae on an industrial scale for mosaics throughout southern and western Britannia as did those in the Forest of Dean. Indurated chalk and limestone equally was transported long distances. Artificial colours were produced by roasting or staining and reused tile and pottery also produced a range of shades. Occasionally evidence of miscalculation of numbers of tesserae required is apparent in the sudden change of colour in borders.

Prefabrication

Workshop prefabrication of elaborate figurative panels has long been discussed. Instances of parts of important figures like the Hemsworth Venus or the Verulamium Lion being truncated because they were made too large for their frames, or high-quality figured panels such as the superb Dewlish Leopard, Britain's earliest realistic animal portrayal, being set into otherwise mediocre work have suggested it. Prefabrication (the 'indirect method') entailed a reverse cartoon of an image being drawn onto a stout fabric. Tesserae would then be glued into place on the cartoon and the figure assembled. It would then be taken to the mosaic, turned over, and mortared into place. After removing the fabric the panel was grouted in. Some panels may have had fine mortar applied before transportation.

In lifting and cleaning figures from the Littlecote mosaic, restorers discovered a red outline painted onto the back of Persephone's tesserae. This suggested the panels were

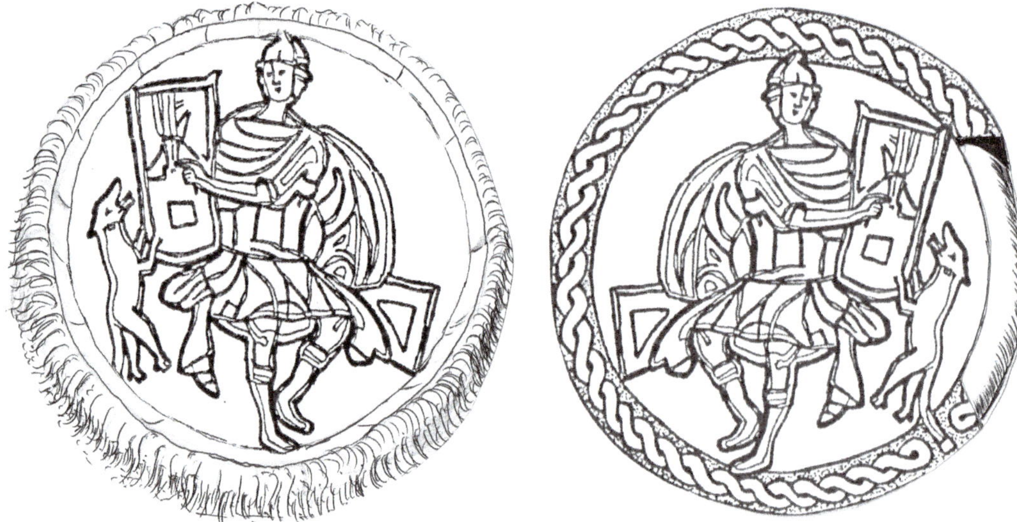

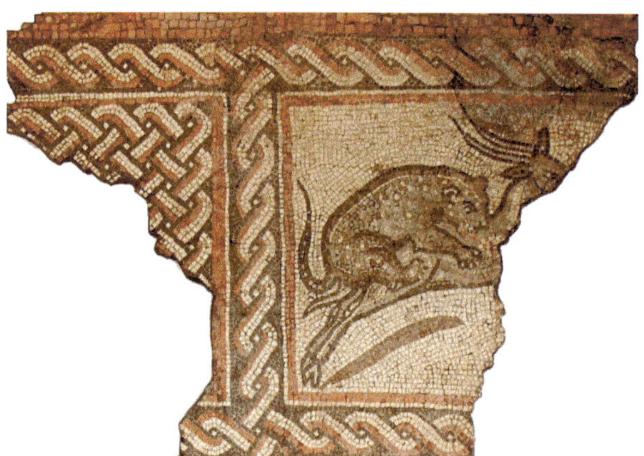

Above: Evidence suggests that Newton St Loe's central panel was prepared by the indirect method and transported to site as a slab. The guilloche border was then added. (Author)

Left: The Dewlish Leopard and Gazelle, Britain's earliest realistic animal depiction and the work of a master figurative mosaicist. Bought for the nation in 2021 and now in the Dorset County Museum, Dorchester. (Author)

produced by the indirect method and to avoid wrongly placing the images in the design, as sometimes occurs when the upper surface was obscured, the outline of the figures was painted onto the panel's back before transfer and setting. Alternatively in Building 1 at Beeches Road, Cirencester, red painted guidelines were found on the mortar of a geometric mosaic. It is possible that guilloche borders might occasionally be ready prepared. As a young archaeologist, Bryn Walters noted that after the Cirencester Beeches Road hare mosaic was lifted there was evidence in the form of a continuous compressed ridge in the surrounding mortar bedding, suggesting that prepared strips of the bordering guilloche had been pushed down into place. While assembling the fragments of the Newton St Loe mosaic the author discovered unique proof of the indirect method on the edge of Orpheus' roundel. This was already suspected as he is too large for the surrounding frame and its crude guilloche border has had to be clumsily altered to accommodate his Phrygian cap. In decay this border has sheared off, exposing an under-layer of mortar with a curious 'poured' appearance like solidified lava. The figure was likely composed and tesserae stuck to a cartoon that was surrounded by a concave clay mould wall. In this case mortar was poured in above the tesserae. When set it was turned over and must have resembled an upturned dinner plate with sloping edges. When stable, this central panel (and presumably also those of the animals) was mortared into place and the fabric cartoon removed. The panels then appear to have been joined together by filling and levelling their sloping sides with mortar on which the crude encircling guilloche and white tessellation were added. All of the pieces of sheared off guilloche retain a negative image of the underlying 'dinner plate' edge on their undersides.

Glass Tesserae and Wall Mosaics

Some mosaics incorporated glass tesserae for added effect. Finds of gilt and other coloured glass tesserae from sites such as Southwick, Sussex, and Keynsham, Somerset, suggest wall or vault mosaics. Many glass tesserae were found at Capel St Mary and Whatfield in Suffolk and they occur widely in London. Otherwise examples of wall mosaics made from ordinary tesserae are rare but certainly existed. Wroxeter's baths boasted guilloche dado borders and a fragment, possibly showing a scroll or *cantharus* handle, was excavated in 2015 from the infilled hypocaust of Room 21 at Chedworth. Some baths were lined with mosaic as at Wingham and Eccles villa (Kent). The latter included patterned steps or a seat. That wall mosaics were desired is suggested by murals imitating them at Sparsholt and Bignor.

3

Coarse Borders

Until the nineteenth century, furniture was generally placed around the walls of a chamber as is illustrated by the sculpted Roman room inside the Simpelveld sarcophagus. Furniture was expensive and historically people stood more, especially in the presence of social superiors. The saying 'the weakest go to the walls' stems from an age when congregations stood in churches

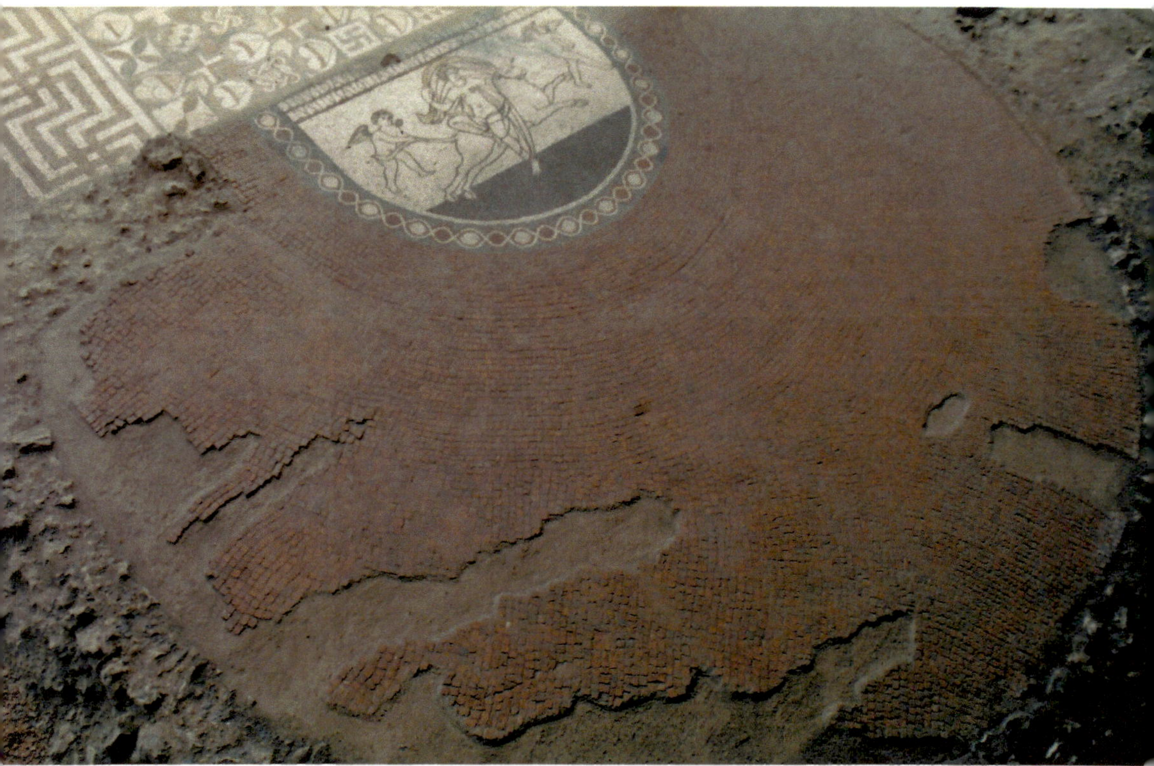

Lullingstone villa's remarkable tessellated apse was designed to accommodate a huge curved *stibadium* dining couch. (Author's photograph)

but benches against the walls, reflecting Roman custom, allowed the old and infirm to sit. Most Roman mosaics reflect this in being surrounded by borders of varying width made of coarse (larger) tesserae in order that the weight and legs of furniture did not damage the finer mosaic. The varying width of coarse borders may hint at a room's ancient use or the position of a lost and important piece of furniture. At Lopen, Somerset, a large rectangular area of coarse tessellation on the eastern side of a grand bipartite reception room either held an impressive piece of furniture such as an *abacus* (sideboard) or the chair of the owner. Similar areas occur at North Leigh (Oxfordshire) and Queen Camel (Somerset). Borders themselves might be plain or could indicate focal points within the room. Room 5 at Rockbourne, Hampshire, has broad red bands that are thought to outline the position of the three couches of a triclinium. Dewlish's Room 4 had a trapezoidal apse with coarse red and white squares perhaps for a dining couch. At Brading the coarse red border of the mosaic in the western, inner, part of the elaborate bipartite reception room incorporates grey T-shaped devices. A separate device rather shaped like the architectural cross-section of a vaulted hall and holding an apotropaic swastika marks where the master's chair would have stood. He faced a panel depicting Perseus

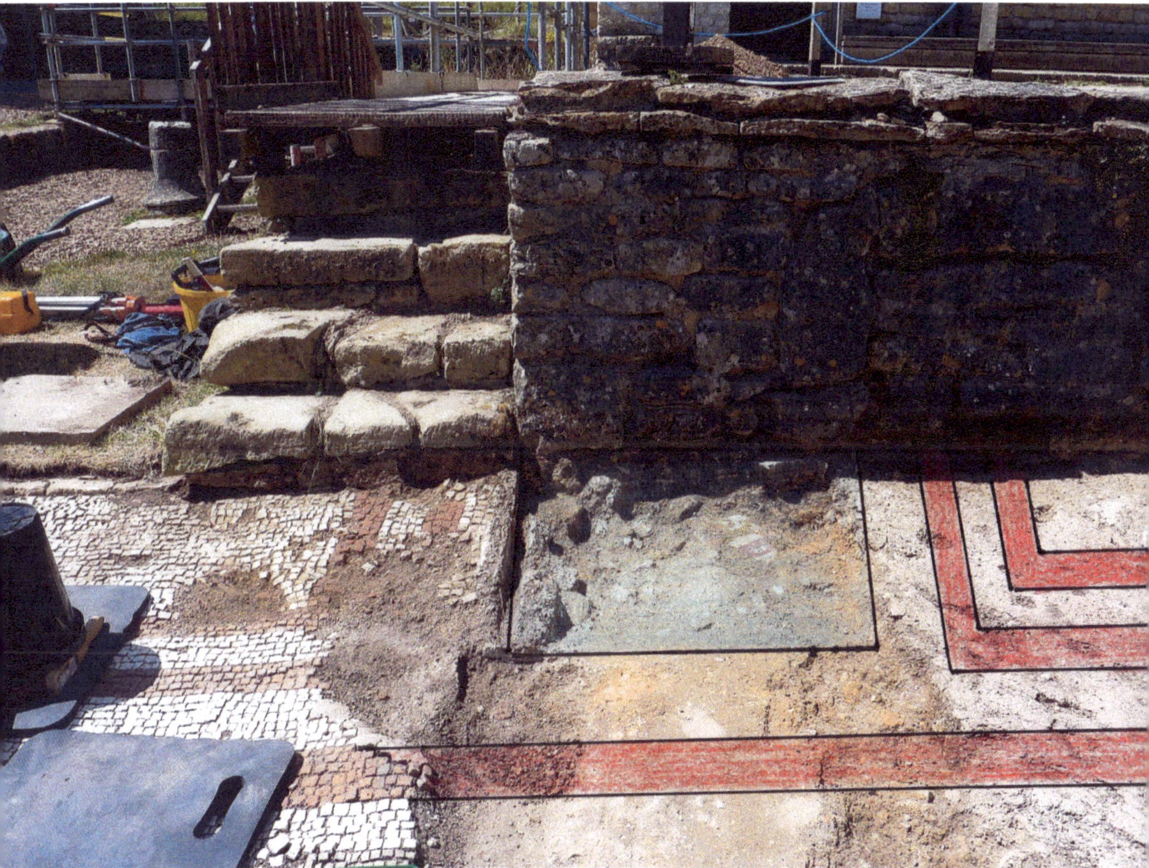

Author's interpretation to explain why the red lines of the coarse border surrounding the huge mosaic of Chedworth's Room 25b turn outwards in order to frame a focal point of the room such as a statue base. (Author's drawing; photograph Nick Humphris)

showing Andromeda the reflection of Medusa's head, the latter again an apotropaic charm against ill luck. Recent excavations led by Martin Papworth and Nancy Grace in the impressive hall (Room 25b) next to the north baths at Chedworth have disclosed the remains of a great mosaic unfortunately badly damaged by Sir Ian Richmond's wall-chasing excavations of the 1960s. The coarse stone border held three bands of red tesserae. The narrower outer two uniquely turn out of the design in the centre of the western side. The author's on-site suggestion was that the turn was to frame and delineate an important feature such as a statue base that it was designed to respect and was the focal point of the room. The wider inner band would have run in front of it while the lesser red bands framed its sides. Such a base would otherwise have clumsily protruded over the bands. Beneath the spot was an early wall that would have served as a good foundation for a heavy statue that would also have been visible from the central garden through a window above the room's nymphaeum pool.

Some second-century mosaic borders have tesserae of almost the same size as those used in the decorative mosaic. Tile borders were more common than stone then but, where the latter replaced ceramic, frequently a narrow band of tile (often made from the ribbed sides of box flue tiles) still surrounded the entire floor as a keying agent for wall plaster. Red tile borders survive throughout the Roman period especially in stone-poor areas. A remarkable British example is at Lullingstone where the huge area of red tessellation paving the apse overlooking the Europa mosaic was designed to accommodate and provide access to a great C-shaped *stibadium* couch.

Simple patterned floors made entirely of coarse tesserae existed. These could be particularly attractive when tile contrasted with stone as a chequered example from Room 7 at Druce Farm, Dorset, shows. Such hard-wearing mosaics were particularly suited for corridors and porticus floors, the designs for which require a study in themselves.

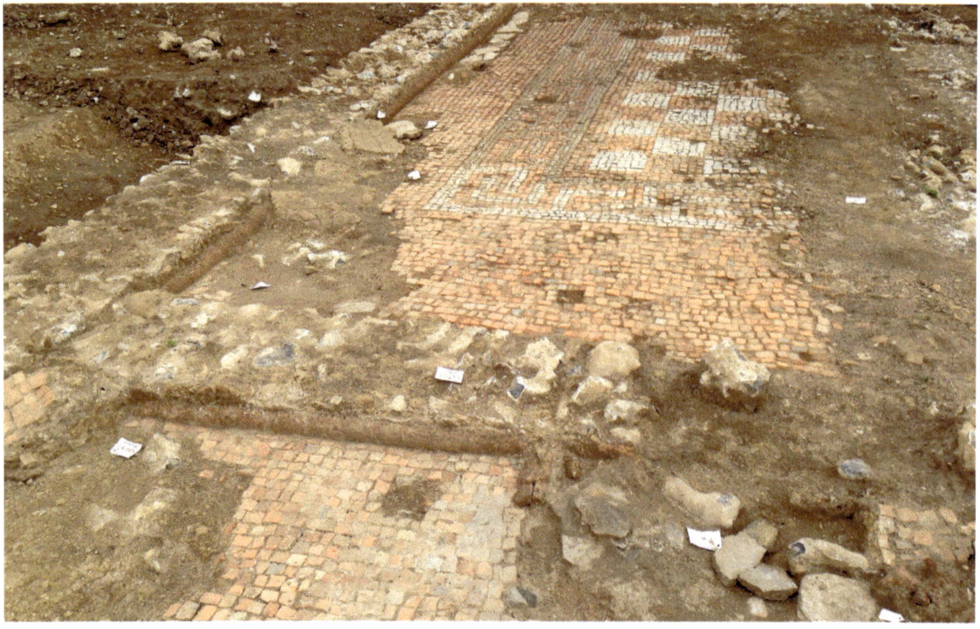

Simple but attractive tessellated pavements in rooms N6 and N7 at Druce Farm, Dorset. (Author's photograph)

4

Sources of Images: Pattern Books and Studio Cartoons

Apart from those images derived from the imagination of individual mosaicists, figured subjects are often condensed from well-known works of art adapted throughout the empire in all forms of everyday decoration. Brading's great reception room mosaic incorporated subjects known to us from wall paintings and mosaics from sites like Pompeii such as Perseus and Andromeda or the House of the Vettii's Achilles on Skyros. Britain's mosaics feature a wide range of myths known to patrons from such works as Ovid's *Metamorphosis*, or the constellation myths of Eratosthenes' *Catasterisms*, Pseudo-Apollodorus' *Bibliotheca*, Hyginus' *Fabulae* or Aratus' *Phaenomena*. Generally compositions are condensed to one to three figures in a central panel, although some mosaics at villas like Brading or Keynsham might have designs featuring many such panels.

Whether mosaicists had pattern books that they could show to clients and use in the planning of commissions has long been debated. It seems logical that something of the

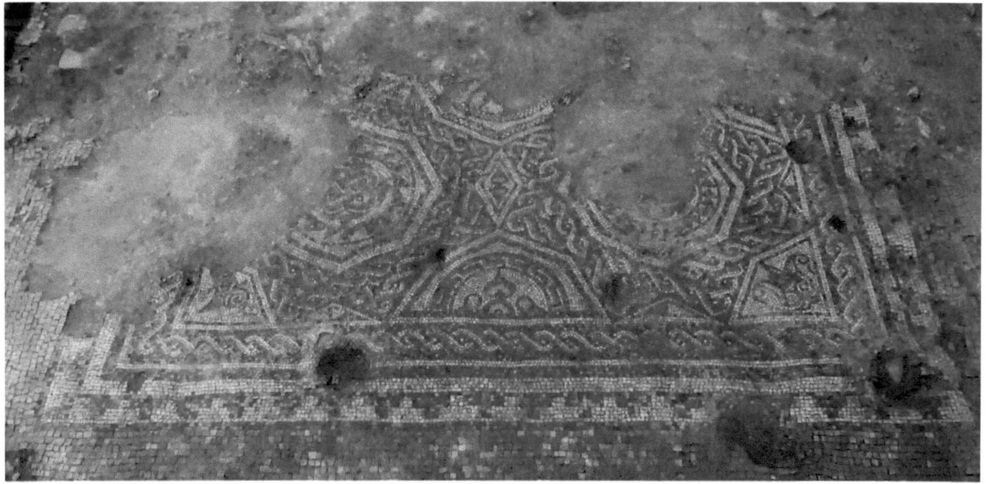

A new fourth-century mosaic featuring interlaced squares was discovered at Bratton Seymour, Somerset, in 2017. (Author's photograph)

kind must have existed if simply for the mosaicists' convenience. Many motifs occur throughout the empire but most mosaicists had their own way of interpreting them. Thus when these unique variations occur elsewhere it is possible to suggest that the same craftsmen/firm were involved. A lost mosaic at Fifehead Neville (Dorset) had a damaged central bust depicting either Minerva or Bacchus. It featured distinctive guilloche knots with lotus flowers growing from them and unusual terracotta foliage. The same lotus knots feature on a fourth-century mosaic with interlaced squares recently discovered at Bratton Seymour, Somerset. This also features a fragmentary naked female bust (probably Venus) wearing a necklace within a central speckle-bordered roundel. Terracotta leaf shapes near the face recall Fifehead Neville's bust. Elements of this new mosaic, together with another of Diana at Bratton Seymour, now link with mosaics at Hemsworth, Dorset, Yatton, Somerset and Bromham, Wiltshire.

With figure work, recurring traits are often found in successive mosaics. The animals and acanthus scrolls of the Corinian Orpheus mosaicists are so similar that they must have been derived from the firm's cartoons. Likewise a trait of some mosaicists connected to the Durnovarian firm was to give its humans dimpled or cleft chins and animals concertina-like muscles to their upper forelimbs, which makes their work distinctive.

Clients would surely have had an input and perhaps shown the mosaicists illustrations of desired subjects from illuminated manuscripts for specific commissions. Some images like Achilles on Skyros were widespread and the mosaicist should have needed no explanation

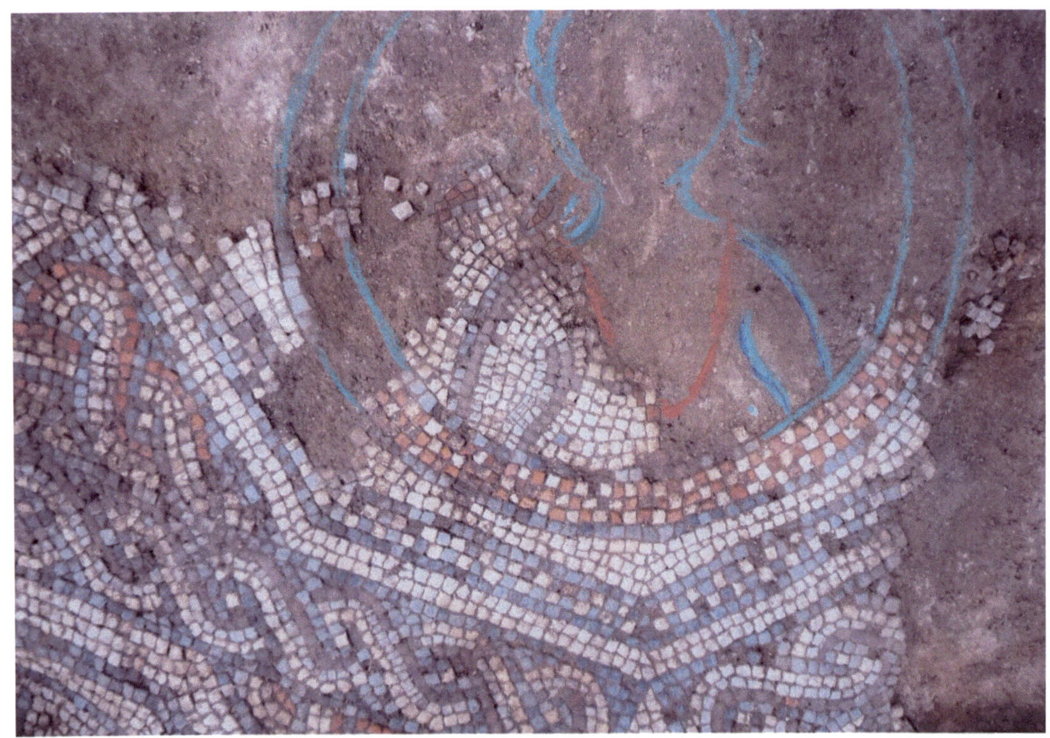

Remains of a possible bust of Venus wearing a necklace at the centre of the 2017 Bratton Seymour mosaic and author's suggested interpretation. (Author's photograph)

as to their appearance. The sophisticated Boxford mosaic, however, with its rare and linked mythological subjects so carefully chosen by a cultured client and possibly drawn from an illuminated codex would have. The same may be postulated for Low Ham's Dido and Æneas mosaic and Horkstow's Medallions Mosaic. Certainly where inscriptions occur, these were surely dictated. Although scholarship seeks deeper meanings for the choice of images on floors, we can never know what was in the client's mind in commissioning a subject. Religion permeated all levels of Roman life and society but what may seem to have deeply religious meanings and connections may, as at Brading, equally be simply a random collection of copies of favourite paintings or stories. Much is made of mistakes in the geometry of mosaics but it is doubtful if, faced with a riot of decoration, the client even noticed or cared that one corner of a large mosaic differed from another any more than a modern householder critically studies the pattern of a carpet.

Uniquely, a possible mosaicist's practice sheet or aide mémoire was excavated in 2013 at a quarried-out Roman settlement at Kingskerswell in Devon. Both sides of a fragmentary slate tablet retain three sophisticated compass-drawn mosaic designs based on intersecting circles with roundels containing six-petal rosettes. One roundel is bordered by six spindle-shaped devices. The engraving is finely executed and not simply a doodle. The petals of one design have dividing lines and are interspersed by six inward-facing, knob-handled leaf fans as appear on mosaics at Lydney and Fifehead Neville. All have thickened volutes and stamen-like points. The tablet's patterns cannot be designs for chip carving as the leaf fans would not be present if this was the case, but they are exactly what one might expect from the hand of a mosaicist. Could this slate fragment be an example of

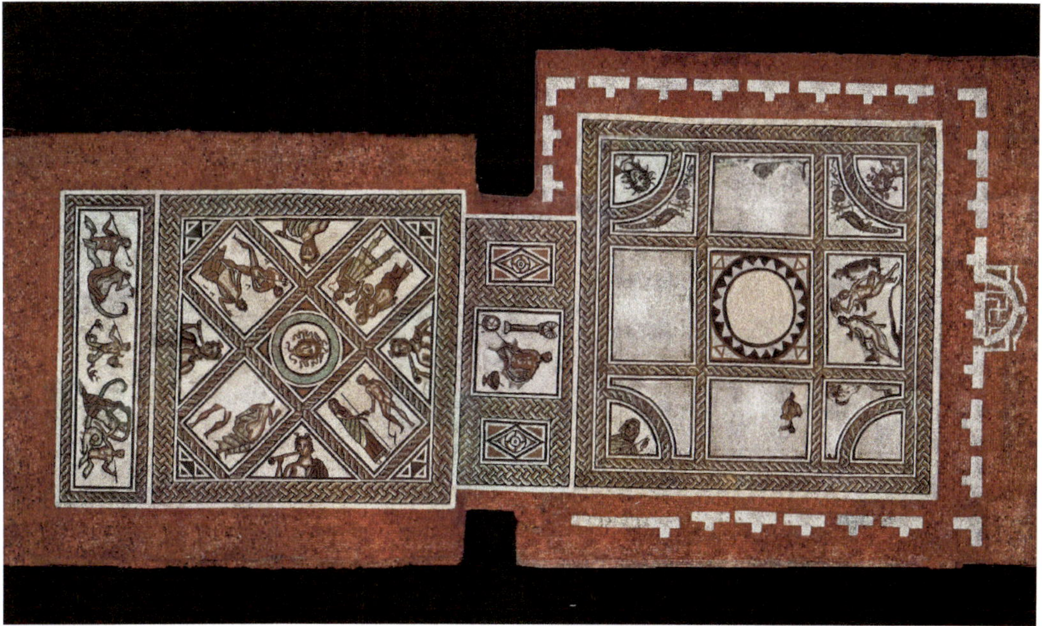

Coloured plan of Brading villa's wonderful reception room. It features a host of panels taken from well-known myths and artworks. One of Britain's premier sites to see mosaics. (Courtesy of David Reeves: Friends of Brading Roman Villa and ORT)

a pattern for a mosaicist engaged on a commission at a site, or even intended to show the design of rosettes to a client?

If so, it is a remarkable and often postulated item, but one that has previously not been identified. Devon has so far produced few mosaics, although sophisticated examples existed at Holcombe villa and at Exeter. Mosaics featuring overall designs based on intersecting circles are not rare in Britain but large-scale designs such as these are. They cannot be exactly matched by any known local pavements but a corridor or porticus mosaic from Pancras Lane, Exeter, and a related one from Somerleigh Court, Dorchester, also feature rows of very large spindle-edge circles. A mosaic from Rampisham, Dorset, featured a central twelve-petal rosette. Many geometric patterns appear to have originated in the elaborate coffering found in monumental architecture such as on the temple of Bacchus at Baalbek. Although seemingly complicated they are often surprisingly simple to construct. Occasionally mosaicists developed their own geometric designs rather than slavishly following the norm. Kingsweston's mosaic is one and another remarkable example is the late fourth-century apsidal mosaic at Badminton with its unique motifs and geometry. Visitors were led down set routes in some houses and those corridors might be elaborated with inset geometric or figurative panels to impress them.

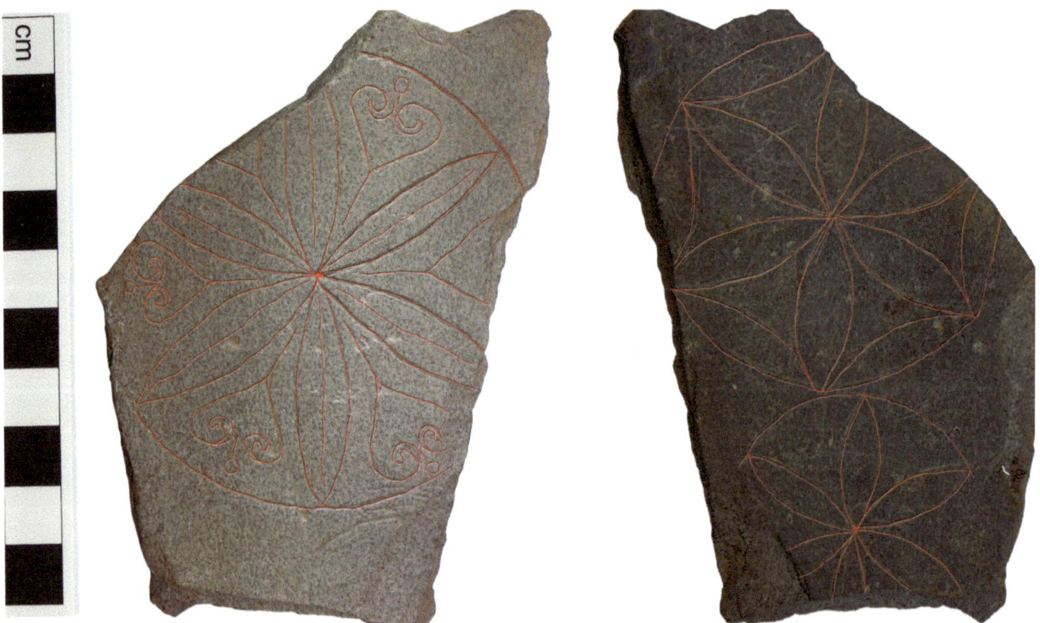

The Kingskerswell slate tablet inscribed with compass-drawn mosaic designs may link with mosaicists working in Dorchester and Exeter. Red highlighting added by the author. (Courtesy of John Valentin, AC Archaeology)

5

Replacing Mosaics: Repairs and Making Do

Redecoration, change of fashion, damage from furniture, or the structural failure of a mosaic often resulted in a new pavement replacing the original. Most commonly this merely entailed laying a new floor directly over the original, much as householders in recent times often did with linoleum. Fishbourne provides several examples of this, notably in Room N7 (the famous Cupid on a Dolphin mosaic) and N13. Possibly some tesserae were recycled where possible, as pick marks existed on the mortar base of the earlier mosaic in Room N7. At Druce Farm villa the author noted rare evidence that the original mosaic in Room N10 had been completely grubbed up and only survived at the north-west corner of the room below the borders of the later mosaic. The latter's mosaicists mixed many of its predecessor's fine tesserae into the mortar of its base.

Damage to mosaics from subsidence, mortar failure or furniture legs often occasioned repair rather than replacement. Such repairs make a fascinating study in themselves and often are indirect evidence of the longevity of civilised occupation and attempts to maintain standards. The original mosaicists were generally no longer available when problems occurred and so others had to assist. Frequently the jobbing builder called upon to effect repairs found it beyond his skill to match even simple geometry. Pattern blindness seems to have been prevalent even if the same colours were used in the repairs. At Woodchester, Room 18's mosaic was patched by a mediocre mosaicist who managed to follow the original geometry but, baffled by the guilloche border, replaced it with a string of solid lemon-like devices. In the northern porticus an incompetent repaired the damaged panel and border with broad bands of red, white and blue. Such bungled interventions occur widely throughout the empire, suggesting that many patrons were more concerned with functional repairs rather than with their appearance. On large, complicated mosaics even bungling repairs might not be immediately evident. Unlike cupboards and chests, dining couches, beds and chairs would have constantly exerted moving pressure on mosaics. Room 1 at Druce Farm displays a series of repairs in the area where a couch probably stood. Primary repairs in reused tesserae followed the existing rows but not their ashlar pattern. At least two later repairs used large darker tesserae and disregarded both pattern and the original rows. There the replaced couch would have hidden the repairs. Eventually, when repair was impossible, patrons patched floors with mortar or, lacking that, with slabs. Druce Farm and Rockbourne had stone roof tiles neatly fitted into missing cavities. Such patching is commonly found, a further example being the frigidarium mosaic of Chester's Fortress Baths.

In rare cases when the repairing mosaicist's work was far superior to the original, as occurs with the bust of Winter on the mediocre Seasons mosaic from Toft Green, York, the result can be just as unsettling. Although iconographically inaccurate in portraying an undraped Winter, the replacement bust there is one of the finest and most sensitive on British mosaic.

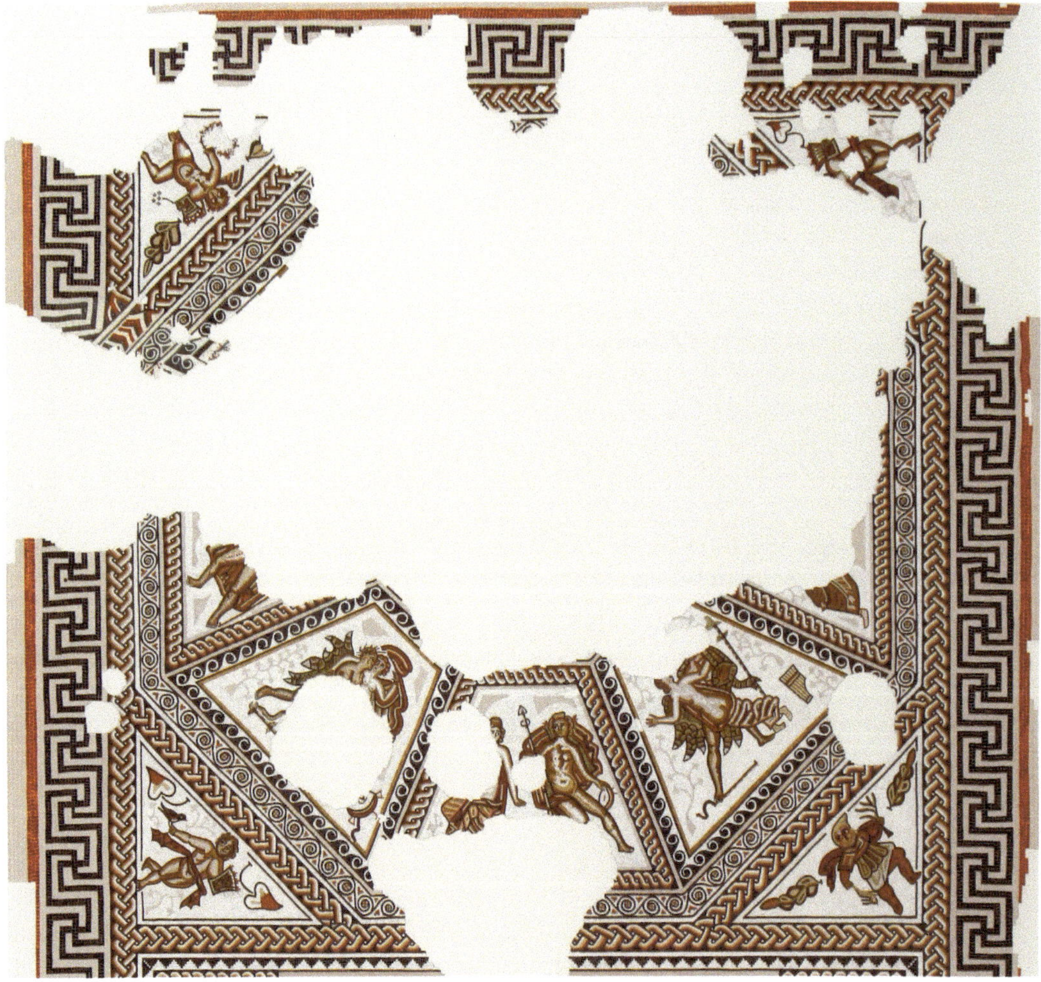

Repairs below the figure of Summer at the top left corner attempted, unsuccessfully, to follow the design of Chedworth's Bacchic mosaic. The outer guilloche of the octagon now intrudes across the mosaic's swastika meander border as a row of chevrons. (Copyright and courtesy of Luigi Thompson)

6

Other Flooring Types in Britannia

Beaten earth, clay and gravel formed the most basic of Roman floors followed by those formed of stone slabs or tiles. However, wooden boarded floors were also widespread and may have covered some of the earthen floors mentioned in excavation reports. In the colder northern and well-wooded regions of the empire, wooden planks either suspended or laid directly on the soil provided an inexpensive, easily achieved, replaceable and, paradoxically, a more comfortable flooring than many of the more expensive masonry alternatives. Panels of the 'woven' guilloche pattern found on mosaics may ape actual rush matting used on Roman floors.

Plain Tessellation

Floors of plain tessellation grew in popularity at the end of the first century. They were presumably less costly than decorated floors but were still an expensive investment and a status symbol. Tesserae were often larger than those used on decorated mosaics and made from reused roof and flue tiles, together with pottery such as Samian ware. The latter's use can assist in the dating of pavements. Plain tessellation floored areas of heavy footfall and, like coarse borders, could be hard wearing. A photograph taken at the Wheelers' Verulamium excavation in September 1933 shows a student worker (wearing heels) giving a tessellated floor a good stiff brushing with a bass broom. To make such floors visually more interesting mosaicists often added the odd tesserae in a different colour. At Druce Farm villa, Room 6 is floored entirely with red tesserae. However, its mosaicists treated it as though it was an ordinary decorated mosaic providing centrally a rectangular panel of slightly smaller red tesserae, surrounded on each side by borders laid to run in different directions, thus subtly emphasising the 'finer' central area and perhaps delineating the positions of couches. The room boasted a masonry brazier stand and may have been a winter triclinium. Otherwise plain tessellated floors in corridors and minor rooms might be boldly enlivened with wide stripes in a contrasting colour, sometimes bizarrely placed as at Dewlish villa. Stone tesserae superseded ceramic in many areas but the latter did not die out.

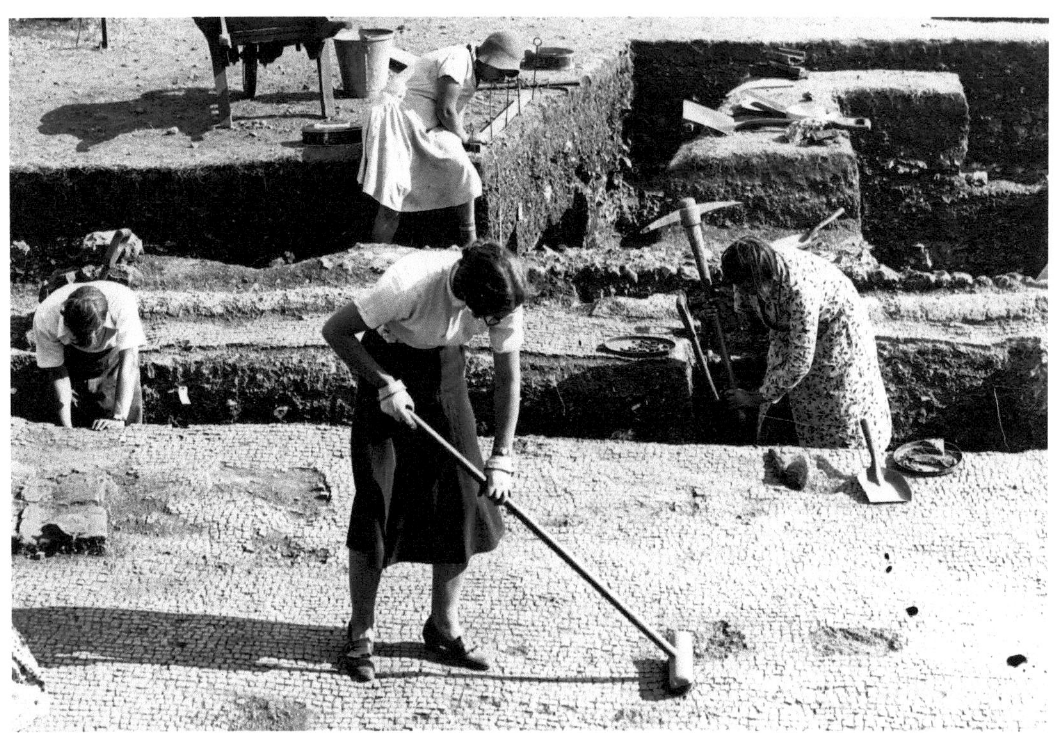

Around a hundred female students excavated at Verulamium with Tessa and R. E. 'Mortimer' Wheeler. Here one demonstrates the durability of second-century plain tessellation with a yard broom on 8 September 1933. (Author's collection)

Alternatives to decorative mosaic or plain tessellation were available. Like mosaics, these would have been levelled and ground to a polish with grinding stones to provide an attractive and easily maintained finish.

Opus Sectile ('Cut Work')

Allied to mosaic was *opus sectile*, an attractive, hard-wearing luxury flooring that employed shaped segments of imported coloured marbles or local stones to form geometric or stylised naturalistic panels. Popular in Italy during the first and early second centuries AD and, by the fourth century enjoying a revival, it was employed in a number of Romano-British buildings both in town and country. Early villas such as Fishbourne, Folkestone and Angmering have yielded elements from destroyed pavements as did Rivenhall and Fingringhoe in Essex. Woodchester's fragments and their mortar share close similarities with Fishbourne's and hint at an earlier lavish Flavian or Trajanic predecessor to the fourth-century palatial establishment. One octagon from Angmering of Sussex marble (a stone notable for polishing well) was 0.3048 metres across and no doubt formed the central element of a panel. Littlehampton museum conserves other segments from its floors. Native stones or tile seem to have been mostly used in Britain and, where

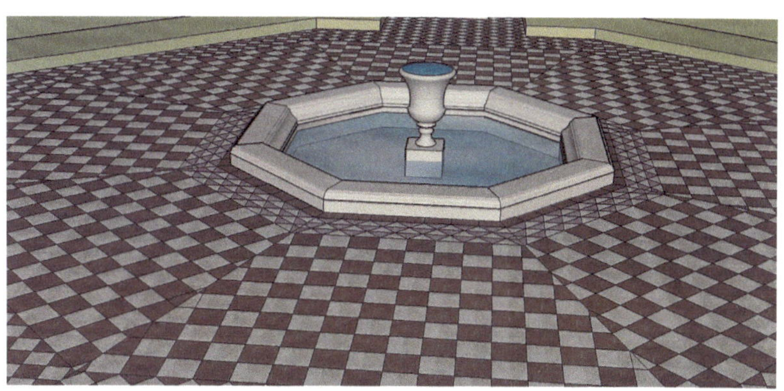

Reconstruction of Great Witcombe's *opus sectile* pavements based on Lysons' recording of the remains. (Copyright David Rider and Bryn Walters)

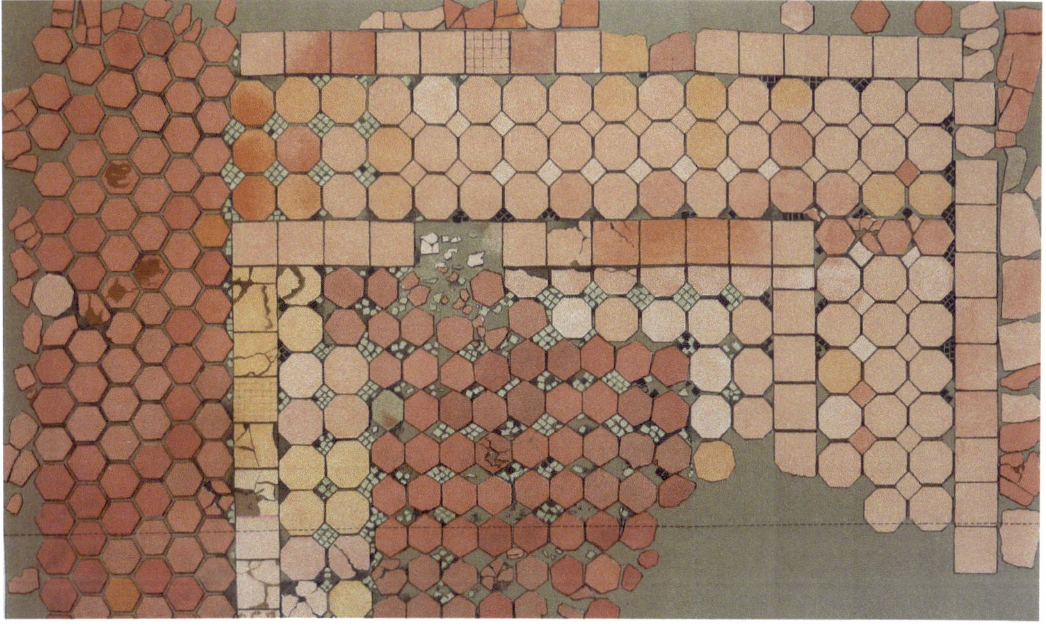

Part of a tile vestibule *opus sectile* pavement from House 1, Insula XXIII, Silchester, as featured in *Archaeologia* 57 part 2, 1901, 230–2 pl xxvii.

imported marbles do occur, it is not always clear whether the pieces were for floor or wall sheathing, as in the case of recent finds at Chedworth and Piddington, although Pit Meads villa (possibly fourth century) had a room floored with polished triangles of white marble. London and other wealthy towns and cities are more likely to have boasted floors featuring imported stones. A fourth-century public building at Culver Street, Colchester, provided sacks of imported elements on excavation in the 1920s including green porphyry leaves. All are now lost. Where marbles were used, it exceeded all other forms of flooring for cost and desirability. Sometimes *opus sectile* pavements could be quite simple such as the Bignor *frigidarium's* black and white chequer board pavement of Kimeridge shale and limestone tiles. A border of red tiles surrounded it.

Samuel Lysons recorded the in situ remains of a fine *opus sectile* pavement that floored the octagonal chamber (Room 15) and gallery (Room 14) at Great Witcombe in Gloucestershire. Probably late third century in date, it is the only British design that can be restored. An outer border of poised chequers held a wide band of chequer work surrounding an octagon of triangles all in contrasting coloured stone. Grey-blue and buff-coloured Lias limestone and Old Red and Pennant sandstone were used. A central pool is suspected in the chamber as at Bignor and a socle from a *cantharus* fountain survives among site finds and is the subject of a forthcoming paper by the author. Other segments from the site in Old Red Sandstone were circular. The chequer work continued along the raised gallery outside the room. Rather than a villa this wealthy, enigmatic site with its underground cult chamber, sets of baths, sacral confronted-S acroteria and abundant water supply, together with its resemblance to the temple complex at Haut-Bécherel, Brittany, suggests a religious complex. Archaeologists Bryn Walters and David Rider have produced a restoration of the Witcombe floors after Lysons' sketch of the remains. Walters has also shown that piles of unusually shaped tesserae from Halstock villa in Dorset may have once formed a *sectile* pavement. Two unusual *opus sectile* pavements floored vestibules at House 1, Insula XXIII and House 2 Insula XXIV at Silchester. The first (now in Reading museum) was composed of tile octagons, later repaired with smaller tile hexagons. The gaps between the octagons were filled with coarse black and buff tesserae. The second pavement was entirely in tile and featured octagons and squares. Both designs are echoed in late Roman marble *sectile* pavements found in two *tabernae* (shops) attached to Rome's Basilica Emilia and fifth- and sixth-century Christian basilicas in the eastern empire.

Mosaics sometimes aped *opus sectile* floors in their geometric designs, possibly hoping to impart a more luxurious feel to a room. At Wingham, Kent, and Braughing, Hertfordshire, the mosaics were composed of lozenges, triangles and chequer work and must have appeared just like a *sectile* pavement as did that from Room 8 at Latimer villa, Buckinghamshire, or those of rooms N4 and N7 at Fishbourne.

Opus Signinum ('Signia Work')

Floors made of pounded brick, tile and pottery mixed with fine mortar were commonly employed in both public and domestic buildings. Waterproof and extremely hard wearing, it often formed the base on which mosaics were laid. The technique was Punic and adopted by Rome, gaining its name from the town of Signia, which was famous for its tile manufacturing. The tile gave the floors a pink or reddish tinge, which, when polished by grinding, produced an attractive finish, aping marble, comparable to the modern terrazzo or cocciopesto floors. Sometimes this finish survives burial as it did in the baths at Pitney, Somerset, assuming 'nearly the polish and consistency of marble'. Polished concrete is easily maintained with the use of clean water alone as wax or oils will dull the appearance, and is far less prone to damage than other forms of flooring.

Punic *signinum* floors often incorporated odd tesserae for decorative effect, either randomly placed or in rows and grid patterns, and this was later copied in early Roman pavements. At Watling Court, London, two early timber houses (built around AD 80 and destroyed AD 120–125) had *opus signinum* pavements with scattered tesserae. Building D there had *opus signinum* floors with black and white crosslets and spaced black and white quartered mosaic roundels reminiscent of Republican Rome's fashion. Possibly these rather old fashioned *signinum* crosslet pavements were commissioned by immigrants from an Italian mosaicist. Building F had a mortar panel inserted into a *signinum* floor bearing a linear arch-like design formed of odd tesserae and perhaps denoting the position of a lost pedestal or altar. Combining *signinum* with mosaic panels is a rarity. The late third-century Curia at Caerwent included a *signinum* floor with an inset T-shaped mosaic panel.

Opus Spicatum ('Ear-of-wheat Work')

Bricks laid in a herringbone pattern to form a floor are also found in some Romano-British buildings. This formed an attractive, hard-wearing pavement that, apart from domestic use as in such villas at Ashtead and Wiggonholt, was often employed in public buildings like the London basilica that had to cope with heavy footfall. At Verulamium an impressive stretch floored the long narrow building 3, Insula IV. Like mosaics the surface was sometimes ground with polishing stones until perfectly level and polished. The *macellum* (market) peristyle and baths at Wroxeter had herringbone paving as did parts of the public baths at Silchester. At Springhead, Kent, Temple 1 possessed a unique late second-century threshold mosaic depicting a poised square between two circular devices in red, yellow and blue tesserae set into an *opus spicatum* pavement.

Painted Floors

One form of Roman flooring that is little known is the painted plaster floor for which evidence does occasionally survive. It had a long history being found in Egypt, Minoan Crete and Mycenaean Greece. A Greek over-painted floor of about 300 BC, aping a mosaic and depicting a prize-winning flautist, survives in Thebes Museum. At Apethorpe villa, Northamptonshire, several rooms were decorated this way, the most impressive having a linear design in red, white and brown. Rooms with lime plaster floors and borders painted with red, yellow and green stripes were also discovered at Nether Heyford in the same county. Other examples are reported at Stanwick, Ilchester, Cirencester and London. Presumably the fresco technique was used on wet plaster so that the colour became embedded within it. These plaster floors would have been polished like wall plaster. It is a reminder that Romans generally wore house shoes such as the *carbatina* when indoors.

7

First-Century
Mosaics in Britain

With the invasion of Britain in AD 43 the army soon constructed permanent bases, and fragments of what may be the earliest surviving British mosaic, presumably laid by legionary craftsmen, come from the Second Legion's baths at Exeter. Tentatively dated to *c.* AD 55–60 it is both figural and polychrome and shows the legion's emblems of a Capricornus (sea goat) confronting Pegasus over a zonal solar globe. Such late first-century AD luxury villas that arose in the south-east of Britain as Angmering, Southwick and Eccles, of which Fishbourne is the nonpareil, all appear to have had mosaics in the fashionable Italian black and white style. Fishbourne's earliest mosaics ornamented the Neronian proto-palace along with floors of *opus sectile.* Later in the century the palace proper was

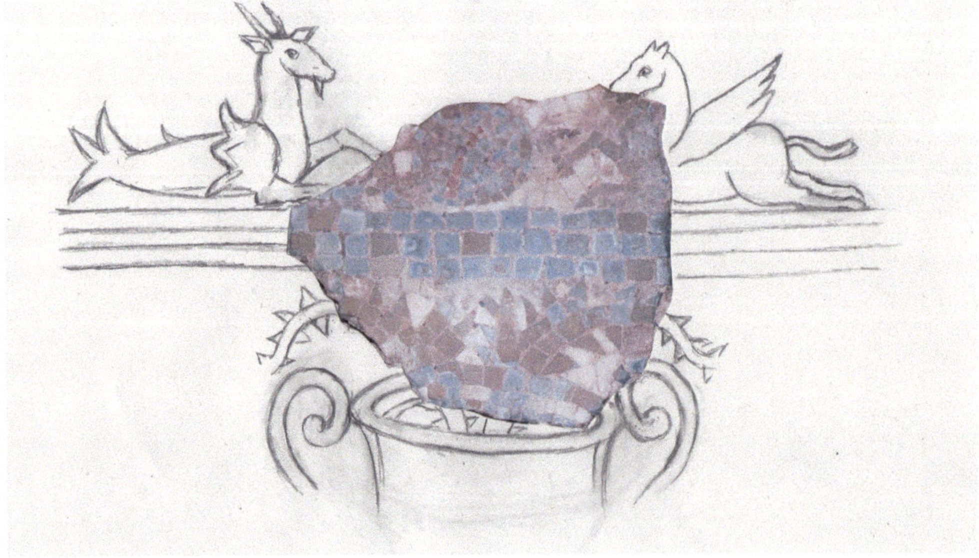

Author's restoration of the very early fragment from a mosaic in the Second Augustan Legion's baths at Exeter. It features the legion's emblems of Capricornus and Pegasus with a zoned celestial globe. Scrolling plants grow from a *cantharus* below. (Author's collection)

ornamented with mosaics reflecting the Italian style fashionable in Gaul. Some included polychrome elements. Most important temples and early public buildings would have had mosaics, sometimes plain white with dark fillet borders, at others grids, often with poised squares and eight lozenge stars. Chichester's first baths boasted mosaics by Fishbourne's mosaicists who must have been kept busy.

London has produced several early mosaics. Late first-century houses in Watling Court yielded rather strange mosaics consisting of odd tesserae or mosaic roundels set into *opus signinum* (crushed tile and mortar) that were oddly old fashioned and might have been more at home in Republican Rome. Another black and white border fragment, however, is matched by Pompeian examples. Building H at this site produced unique British evidence for a mosaic on an upper floor. Gutter Lane produced a white mosaic bordered by a black fillet and with a central black circle enclosing a square. It was surrounded by coarse red tesserae.

Late first- to second-century black and white mosaics occur throughout Britain and reflect Italian taste rather than that of Britannia. Their light chromatic neutrality contrasted well with the rich colours of wall and ceiling paintings so that rooms were not overpowering. There appears to have been some sort of black and white revival in the fourth century when mosaics like that in Room 1 at Druce Farm were laid and such patterns as 'ashlar' enjoyed a limited revival.

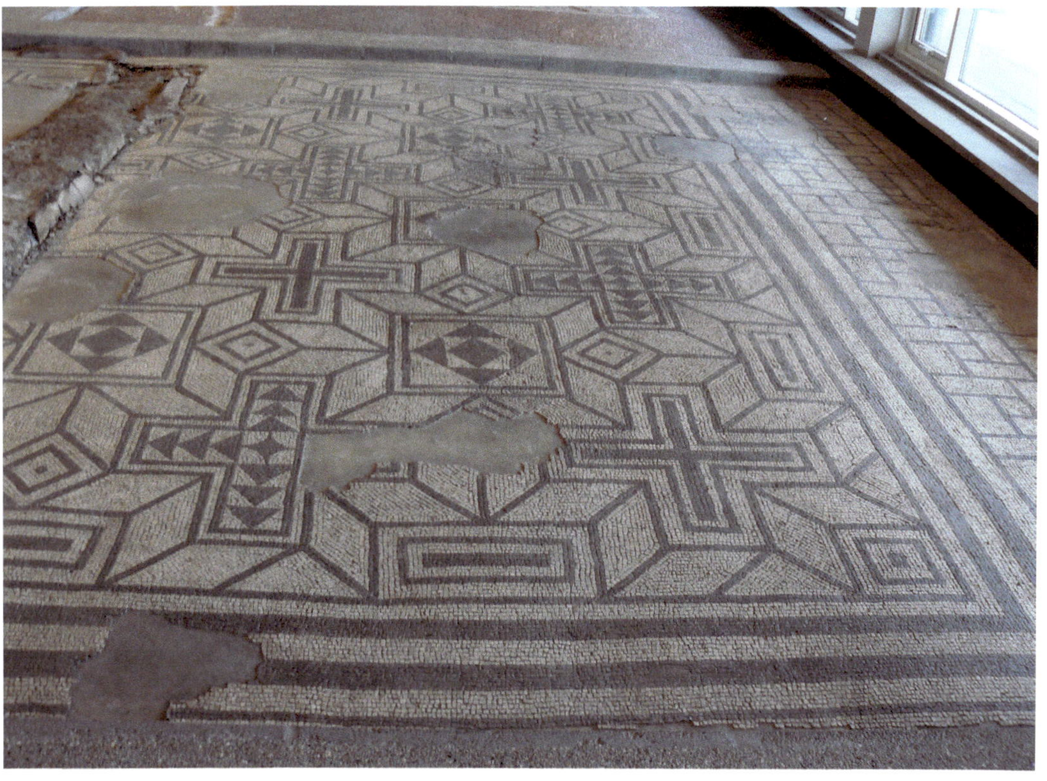

Fishbourne Roman Palace, Sussex, is Britain's finest gallery of early mosaics. This late first-century example from Room N12 encapsulates the Italian geometric style. (Courtesy of Robert Field)

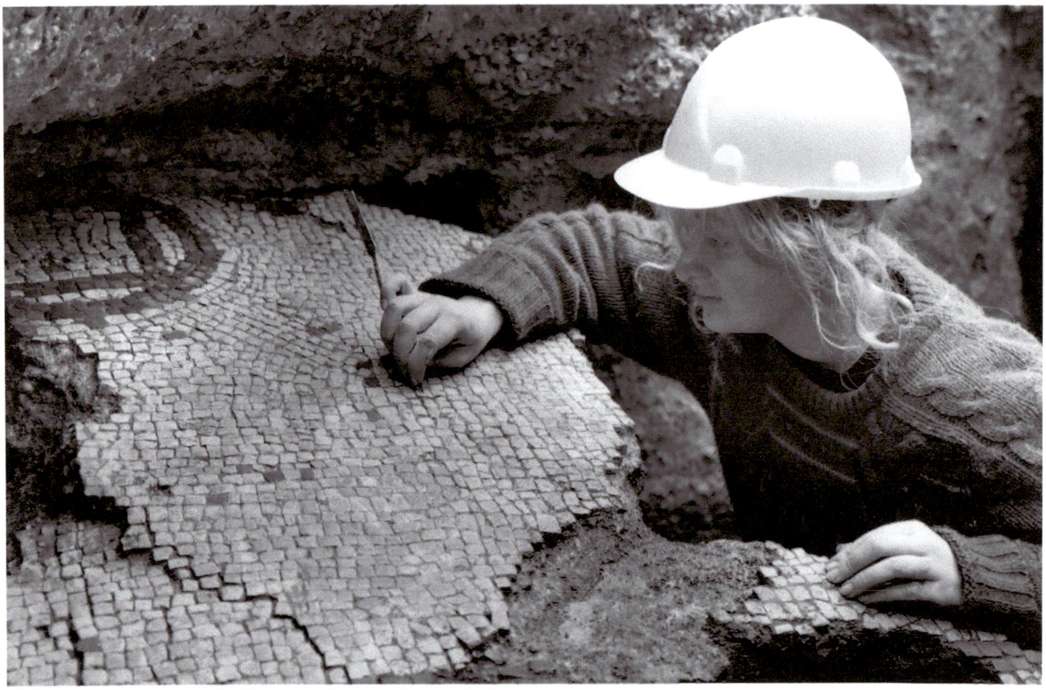

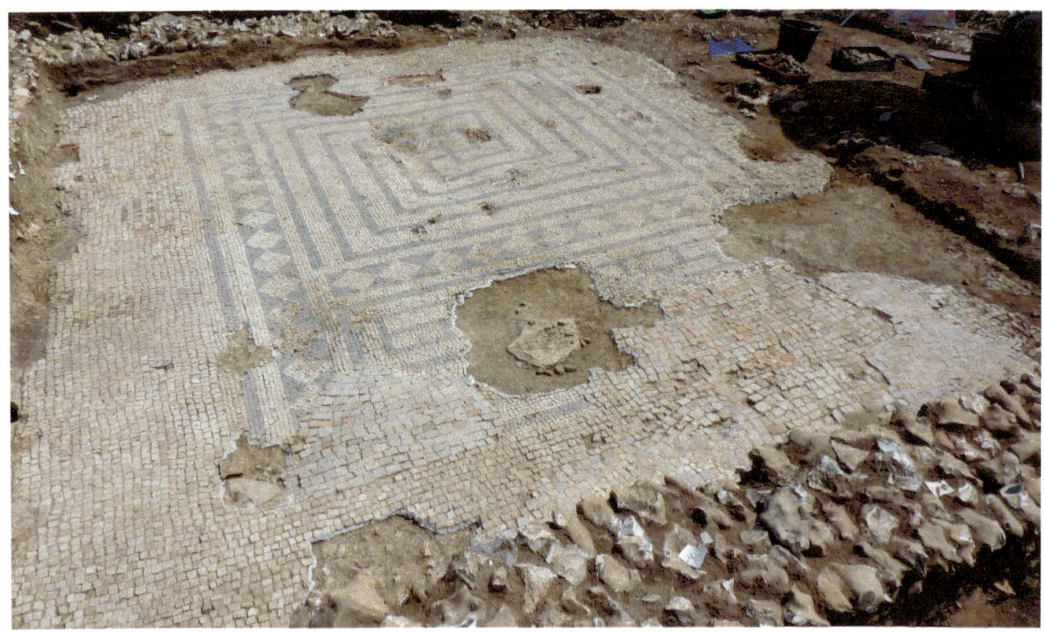

Excavations in London's Gutter Lane in February 1988 uncovered an unusual late first-century black and white mosaic set in a red tessellated border here cleaned by Victoria Ridgeway. (Author's collection)

The recently excavated swastika-labyrinth mosaic from Room 1 Druce Farm, Dorset, displays a fourth-century revival of the black and white style. (Author's photograph)

8

Second-Century Flowering

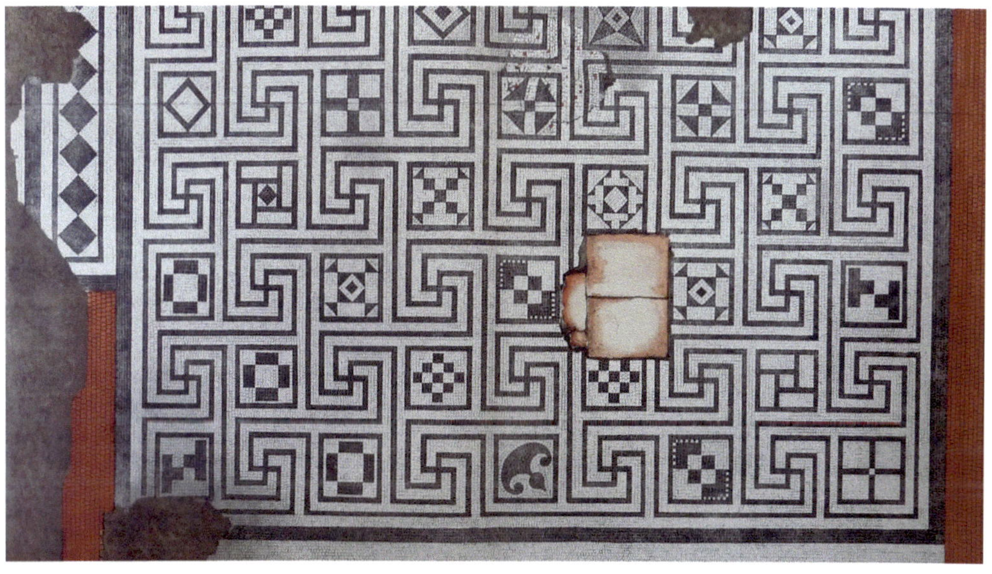

An Italianate mosaic at Silchester that was either old fashioned or incorporated from an earlier property. Note the tile repair. A related pattern was discovered sealed beneath Fishbourne's Medusa mosaic. (*Archaeologia*, 1896, 55, pt 1., 226, plxiii, pl xi)

The second century saw the great expansion of towns in Britannia and an increase in public and domestic building. This generated a desire for mosaics and new firms sprang up to cater for the need. The mosaics of this period are known from towns both in the south and north and the work of several firms can be identified in Camulodunum (Colchester) and Verulamium (St Albans). There are traces of the Verulamium firm's work also in Camulodunum, and there must have been a cross-fertilisation of ideas or a movement of craftsmen. During this century a series of uniquely British designs and variants began to evolve that are rarely duplicated on the Continent.

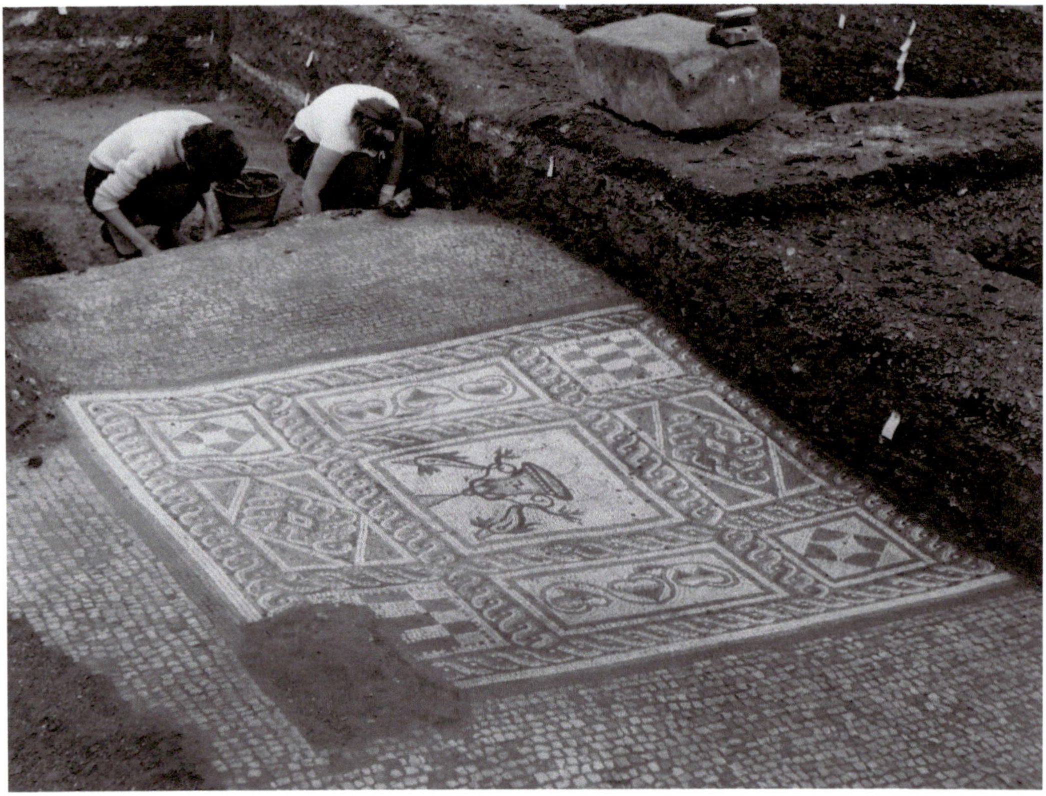

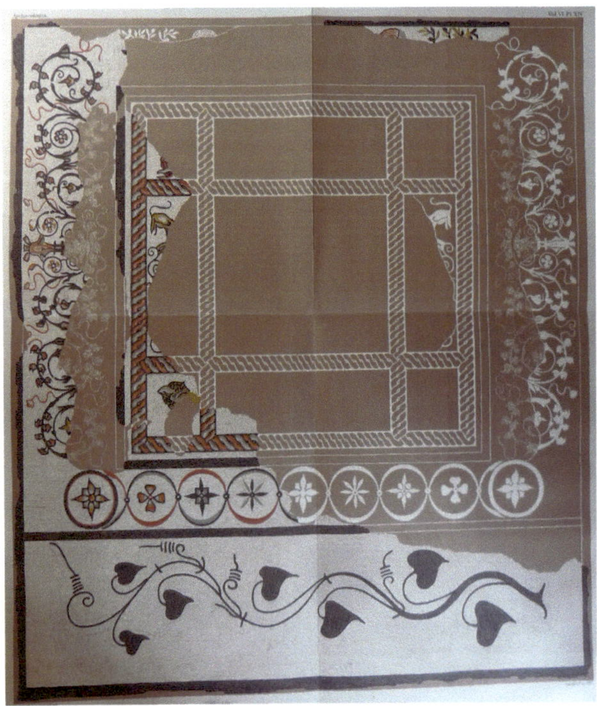

Above: The 1958 Verulamium excavations uncovered a second-century, nine-panel scheme depicting a *cantharus* fountain with dolphins and lotus scroll side panels in Insula XVIII, building 3. (Author's collection)

Left: A nine panel mosaic from Silchester with highly elaborate borders. Leopards flank a *cantharus* and Winds occupy the corners. Most mosaics from the site are now in Reading museum or their store. (*Archaeologia*, 1899, 56, pt 2, 243–50, pl xiv)

Generally second-century mosaics were elegant, elaborately geometric, set in *opus signinum* and well made on firm foundations. Interestingly, whereas black and white based mosaics seem to have continued in popularity in the Mediterranean provinces, polychrome seem to have been the rage in Britain from early in the century. Perhaps the warmth of colour was preferred in the colder north. A notable domestic exception is a black and white meander mosaic from House 1 Insula XIV at Silchester. Related to one later covered by the Medusa mosaic at Fishbourne, it may have survived from an earlier timber-framed house on the site. Notwithstanding their use of polychrome the main field of most British mosaics was white, so they still appeared light against the heaviest of wall decorations. Some public buildings such as Wroxeter's bath-basilica and Lincoln's forum-basilica were still being embellished with Italian-style black and white mosaics around AD 150, perhaps by imported mosaicists on official commissions.

Many geometric mosaics were based on nine panel schemes with a central, often figurative square panel, bordered by rectangular panels and corner squares. The mosaicists in the area of Camulodunum and Verulamium produced some stunning examples. A variant superimposed the guilloche grid of squares and rectangles over an elaborate roundel whose circumference appeared in the rectangular side panels and thus imparted an element of depth to the design. Remarkably, a copy of this south-eastern variant design occurs on a fourth-century mosaic discovered at Yarford, Somerset, in 2003/4. This hints at either a special commission, or another retro-revival of a design. Many mosaics

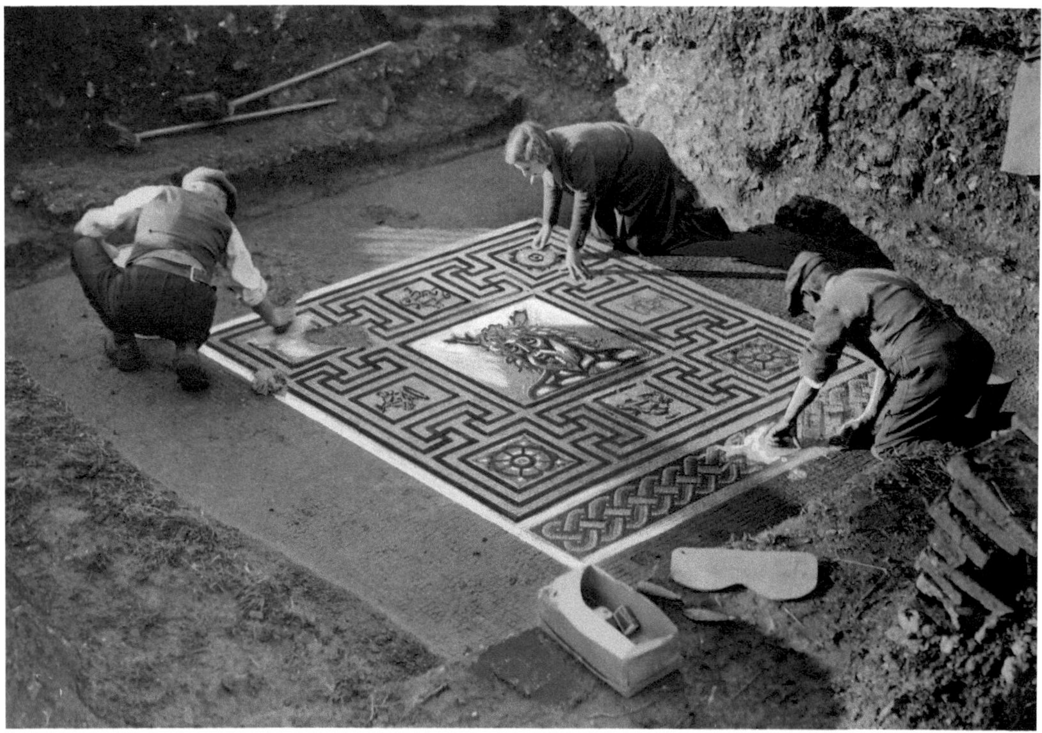

Tessa Wheeler and Italian mosaic restorers working on the Neptune mosaic from Insula IV, building 8, at Verulamium in November 1931. (Author's collection)

incorporated a square rosette into the corner boxes. Although rare on the Continent, it appears on the pavements of the south and south-east of Britain such as the Verulamium Neptune mosaic or that in Chichester Cathedral. Other designs were composed of grids of octagons, hexagons and lozenges. Squares, separated by poised squares, with eight lozenge stars filling the interspaces are also found. Whereas in the south-east there was a fashion for nine-panelled mosaics, in the west there seems to have been a delight in grids

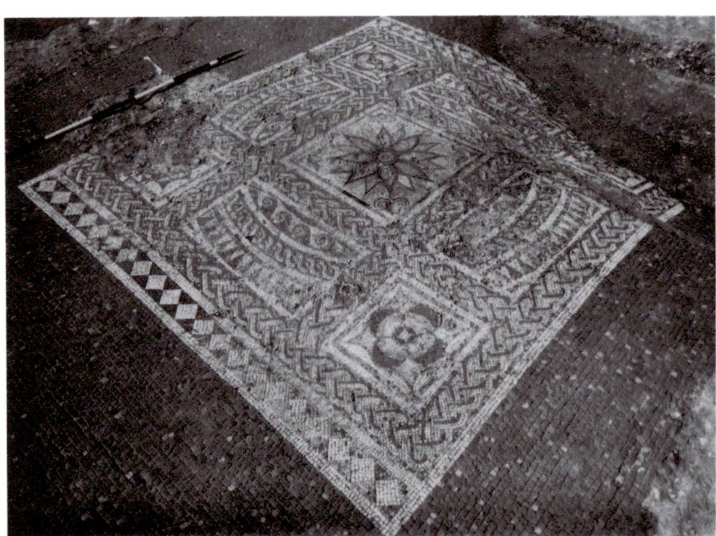

A second-century nine-panel grid superimposed over a circular panel with a lotus centrepiece and squared corner rosettes as discovered at Verulamium in Insula IV, building 1, 1931. (Author's collection)

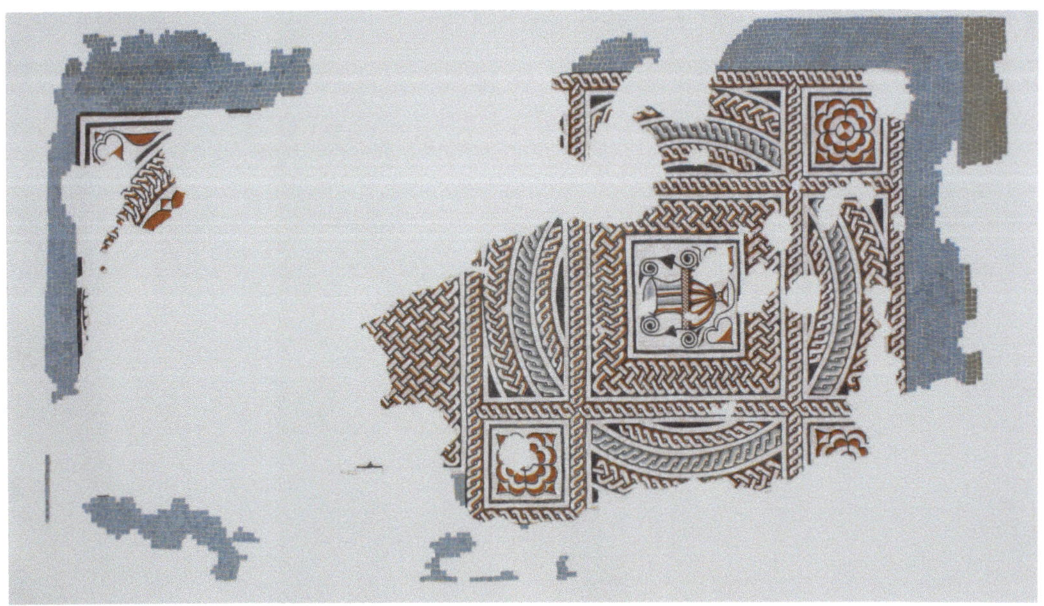

Yarford, Somerset. A fourth-century mosaic aping the second-century design used in Verulamium and Camulodunum. The damaged end imitates an apse within a rectangular design. Drawn by David S. Neal and painted by Stephen Cosh. (Copyright DSN and SC)

of nine octagons. At Great Witcombe, Gloucestershire, the central octagon is occupied by a guilloche-bordered roundel forming a symbolic pool with a *cantharus* fountain and lotus leaves while the others are decorated with whirling devices and perspective boxes.

Ratae Corieltauvorum (Leicester) features some superb examples of geometric mosaics featuring complex octagons, notably the Blackfriars mosaic, the Peacock mosaic from St Nicholas Street (incorporating glass tesserae) and the recently excavated Stibbe factory pavement. The latter consists broadly of a panel of latch-key meander, surrounded by a wide border of confronted *peltae* (Amazons' shields). A grid of nine octagons joins

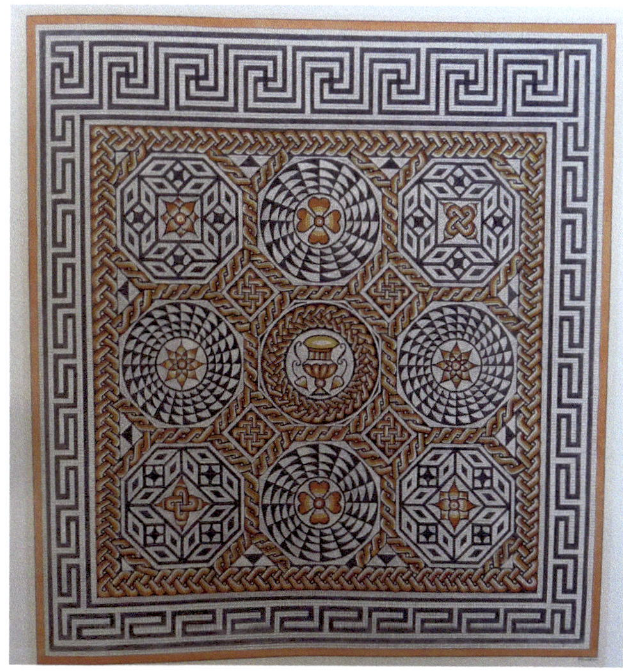

Samuel Lysons' recording of the second-century *cantharus* and octagons mosaic at Great Witcombe, Gloucestershire.

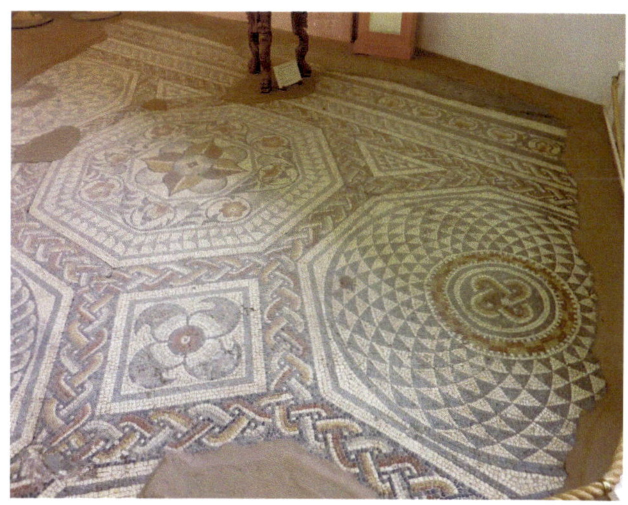

Detail of Leicester's superb second-century Blackfriars, nine-octagon mosaic. Now in the Jewry Wall Museum. (Author's photograph)

this panel. Busts of the seasons possibly occupied the corner octagons while the others held geometric patterns. The remaining one depicts either a cockade fan as at Grateley, Hampshire, or a spoked parasol pattern. The 'fabric' segments are shaded light and dark adding depth. The remaining corner octagon has long-stemmed leaves springing at an angle from a possible head. Like a bust at Brading this may have been Spring crowned with leaves.

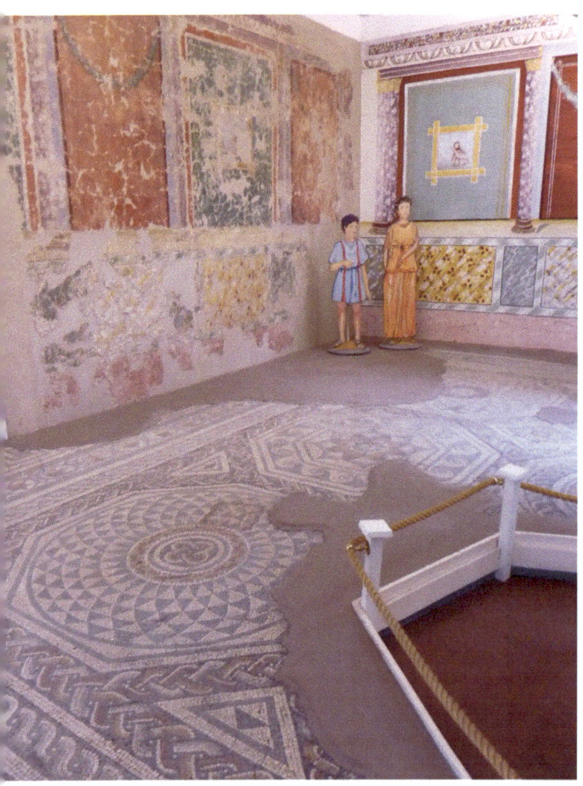

Left: The Blackfriars mosaic exhibited next to original and replica Roman wall plaster to give an idea of how the two media complemented an interior. (Author's photograph)

Below left: The Peacock mosaic from Leicester's St Nicholas Street and in Jewry Wall Museum, incorporated glass tesserae in the 'eyes' of the bird's tail. (Author's photograph)

Below right: Excavating Leicester's Stibbe mosaic in May 2017. The panel of latch-key meander and guilloche knots is bordered by a design of confronted grey peltae within a border of grey poised squares. Part of the grid of octagons appears lower right. (Courtesy and copyright Gavin Speed and UCLAS)

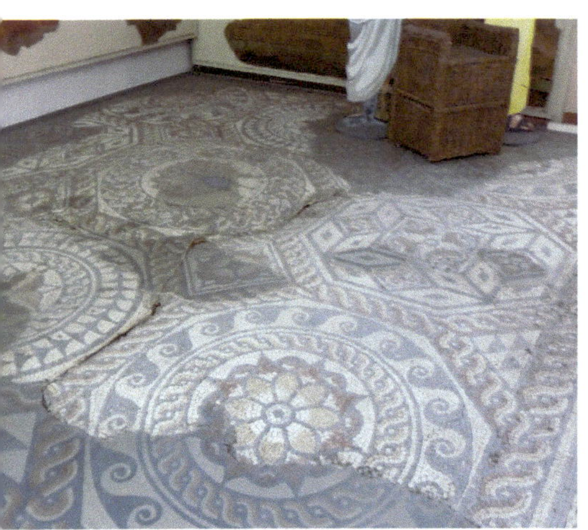

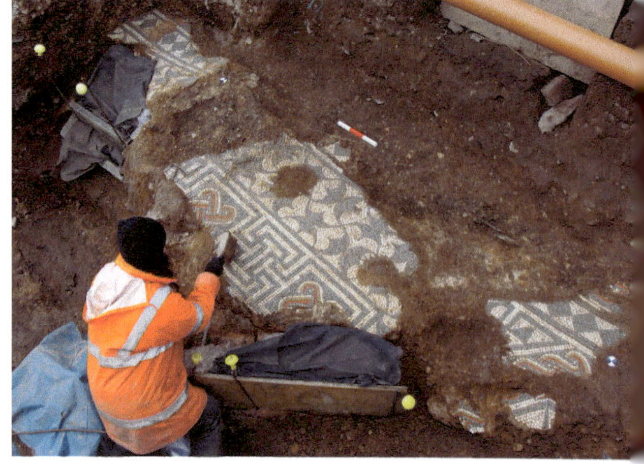

Corinium (Cirencester) has also produced several beautiful figured pavements of this era including the Dyer Street hunting dogs mosaic, Britain's finest marine pavement and a superb octagonal grid pavement. This features the Four Seasons, Bacchus, Silenus, Actaeon and a damaged central panel once featuring Pegasus or Chiron. An elegantly simple mosaic designed for an important public ambulatory around a great courtyard was found at St Michael's Field. It featured a grid of large squares formed by grey fillets with crosslets in their centres and white squares at the intersections.

Designs based on the indented square (actually formed by a grid of circles) became widely popular in Europe during the Antonine era, although a first-century AD example survives at the House of the Tragic Poet, Pompeii. Possibly the design originated for water garden islands and flower beds. It is memorably used in the Hadrianic water garden of the Domus Augustana's lower peristyle on the Palatine and in gardens such as Conimbriga's in Portugal. Occasionally it occurs in architecture of the era such as Bath's 'quadrangular monument'. It offered mosaicists an opportunity to create symbolic water gardens, filling

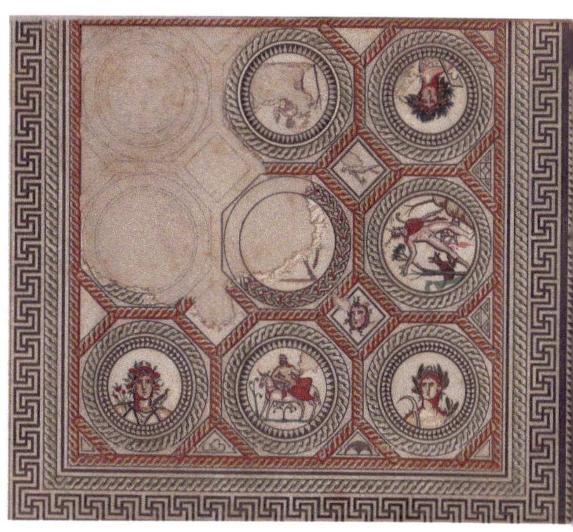

Right: Cirencester's superb octagons mosaic from Dyer Street, now in the Corinium Museum, featured some of the finest figure work in Britain. Engraving by Buckman and Newmarch, 1850. (Author's collection)

Below left: Fragment of an octagons mosaic found beneath the Congregational Church in Dyer Street, Cirencester, in 1972 and now in the Corinium Museum collection. (Bryn Walters)

Below right: Part of the black and white mosaic from an ambulatory connected with a temple or public building and surrounding a vast courtyard at St Michael's Field, Cirencester. Dated to around AD 150–170. Found in 1974. (Author's photograph)

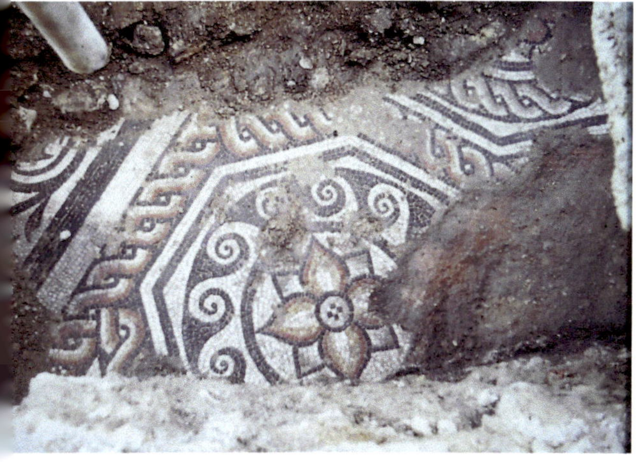

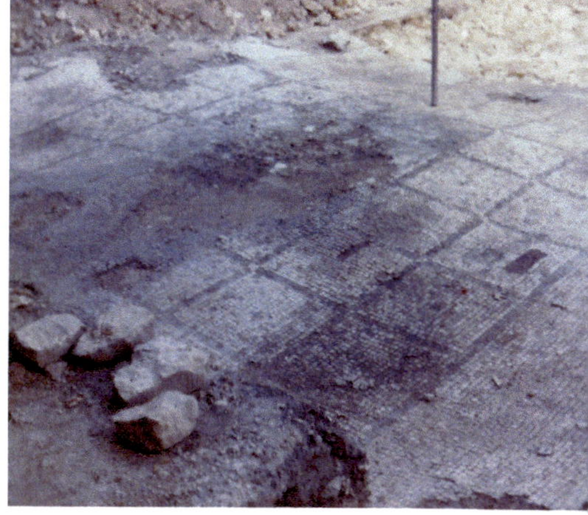

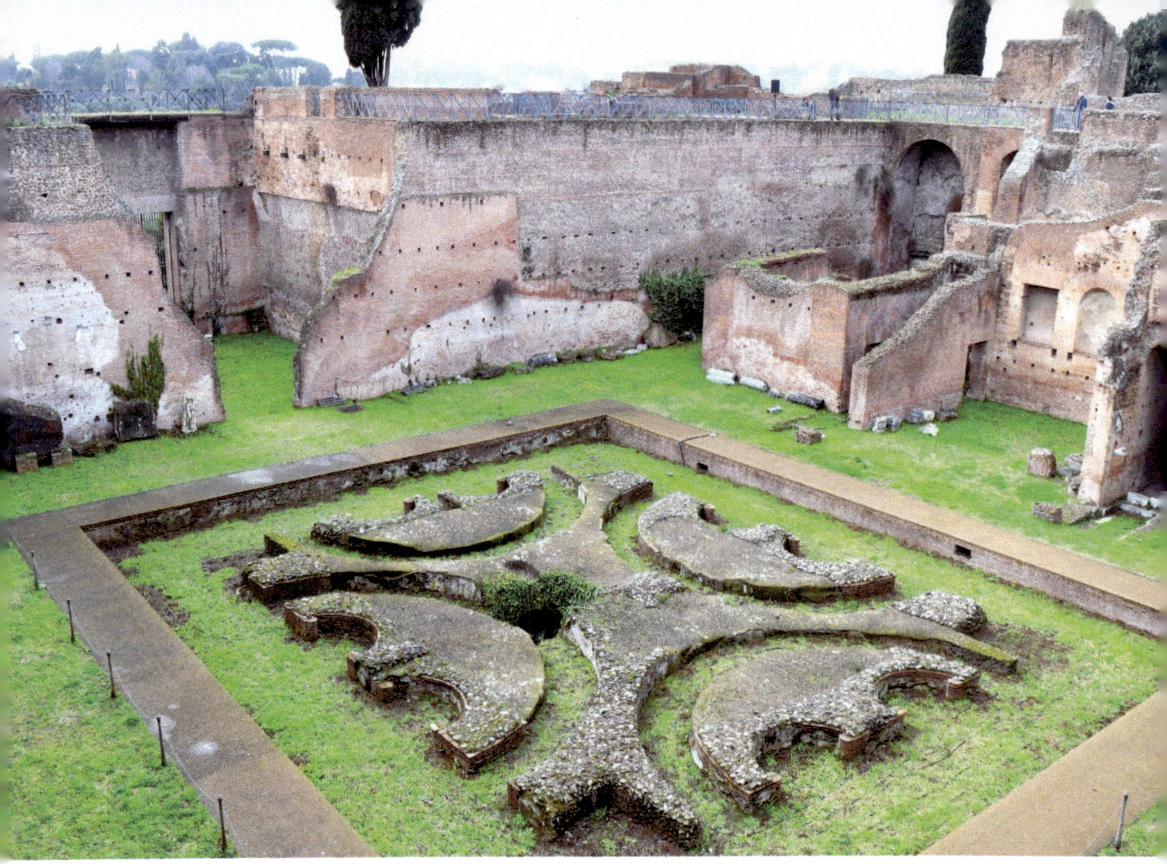

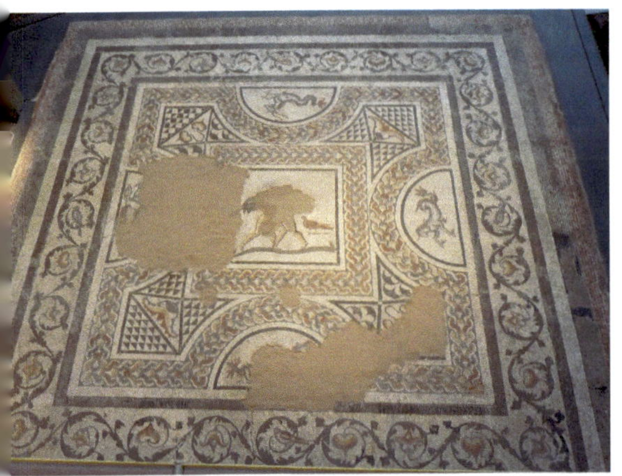

The sunken garden of the Palatine with its indented square and peltae design. (Author's photograph)

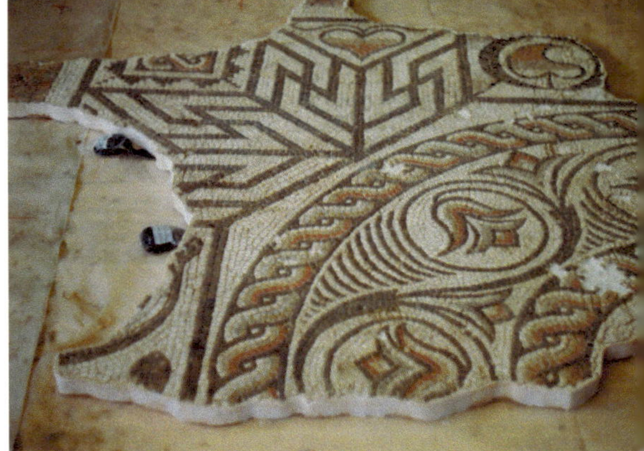

Above left: The exceptionally fine 'Wrestling Cupids' mosaic from Middleborough features an indented square design. Now in the Castle Museum, Colchester. (Colchester Archaeological Trust)

Above right: The surviving quarter of the beautiful second-century Brooks mosaic from Winchester seen here in 1988 during restoration. The concentric circle features a wonderful vegetal scroll with stylised tendrils. Now in Winchester Museum. (Author's photograph)

the indented side lunettes with marine creatures or lotus flowers to enhance the allusion, and a circular or square central panel where the subjects depicted might ape garden statuary or a pool. The lion and stag mosaic from Verulamium offers a good example of this pattern with a square central panel. *Canthari* often stand on the spandrels aping urns or garden fountains. A fine example comes from Middleborough, Colchester, where a damaged central panel depicts the dove of Venus watching either the wrestling contest of Eros/Cupid and Anteros (i.e. love versus requited love) or a version of the group of Cupid embracing Psyche. Popular variants of this design introduced additional corner lunettes as on the Cupid and Dolphin mosaic from Fishbourne or the Vine Street pavement at Leicester. Squares might replace corner lunettes as at Walton Heath. When designs include a central circular panel, these are sometimes referred to as 'nine-panelled compass drawn mosaics'. The indented square design continued in fashion into the fourth century.

Second-century mosaics are rare or not recognised in the countryside but they certainly occur throughout Britain. Examples may be cited at such sites as Ashtead, Folkestone, North Leigh, Hambledon, Coberley, Winterton, Boughspring, Brislington, Great Witcombe, and Well.

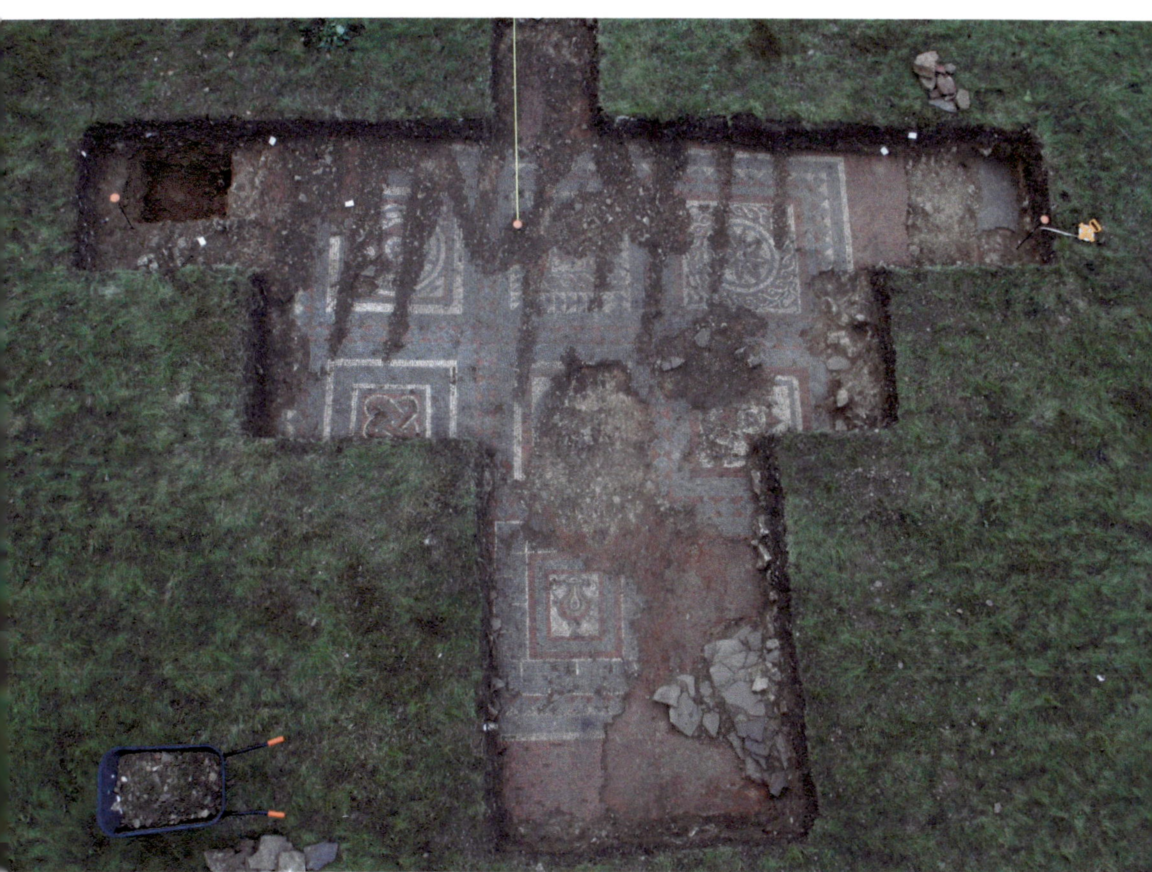

Coberley's second-century mosaic features two *canthari* and bands of poised square decoration as also found at Fishbourne. One *cantharus* displays great artistic ability. An adjoining pavement's border appears top right. (*Time Team*)

9

Third-Century Stagnation

After the vibrant second century the third seems to have been one of stagnation throughout the empire so far as mosaics were concerned. Generally this is blamed on the turbulent political situation, but that can hardly have caused the collapse of an industry all through the several generations of a century. Was there perhaps a change in fashion and that either *opus signinum*, plain tessellation, *opus sectile* or another surface was preferred to decorative mosaic for a while? A basic problem with all mosaics is their dating and much is still guesswork. If they overlie coins or datable pottery then they cannot be earlier than these, but there is no way of knowing how old the former were before they were buried. One reason for the apparent absence of third-century mosaics may be the care with which those of the previous century were generally laid and their subsequent longevity, but new buildings would have been erected and others altered requiring flooring. Alternatively what survives has not been recognised as third century or accurately dated. Received

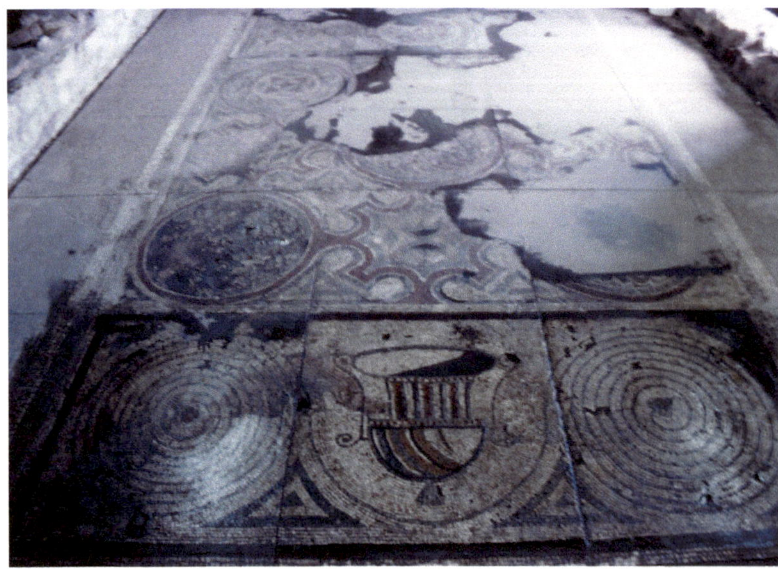

Kingsweston's innovative pavement shows great technical skill. It may date from the third century. (Author's photograph)

knowledge in archaeology can sometimes be a curse and new finds are dropped into convenient second- or fourth-century slots.

A likely reason for the apparent shortage of third-century mosaics may be the catastrophic pandemics (believed to be smallpox) that swept the empire at the end of the second century and the middle of the third. The Antonine Plague of AD 165–180 and the Cyprian Plague of AD 249–262 decimated the empire, killing as many as one-third of the population in some areas and devastating the Roman army. Many towns and villages in the Italian Peninsula and the European provinces reputedly lost all of their inhabitants. It is around this time that the enigmatic abandonment of vici on Hadrian's Wall occurs. It may therefore be the lack of availability of professional mosaicists rather than any change in fashion or despair at the troubles caused by usurpers or barbarians that accounts for the apparent lack of mosaics. As a pandemic is rampant at the time of writing it is quite understandable that commissioning new mosaics must have been furthest from the mind of homeowners at those times even if mosaicists survived the onslaught and could be found.

In the vacuum jobbing builders may have tried their hand at the craft to fulfil any demands and singular or naive mosaics are often assigned to them. Such a piece is Aldborough's Romulus and Remus, three borders of which were reworked by its Victorian owner. The north wing at Fishbourne displays several replacement mosaics that possibly date to the early third century, while Bignor has a naive example depicting Medusa and the Four Seasons. It seems likely that the unique, competently laid mosaic from Bristol's Kingsweston Villa also dates from the third century. It may be the work of mosaicists employed at Venta Silurum (Caerwent) directly across the Severn. Because of the hostility of the Silures, Venta was founded later than other regional centres and a number of its unusual mosaics may well be third century. Bristol's Brislington Villa also possessed mosaics of this date. Leicester's Highcross site yielded a simple red and grey geometric mosaic in 2012 laid over second-century pottery that may also be a candidate. The Orpheus and Medallions mosaics flooring, the huge 18 m x 8 m reception room in the enigmatic complex at Horkstow, Lincolnshire, may well have been laid during the third century. Its sophisticated concentric circles design and iconography based on the shield and life of Achilles, coloured backgrounds together with its message of 'opposites' and love, life and death, enshrine the culture of its patron and designer even if its mosaicists lacked the technical skill to successfully accomplish it. The adjacent Orpheus panel bears a closer relationship to the mosaic depicting him at Volubilis, Morocco (dated mid-third century AD), than to those of the next century. The juxtapositioning of Orpheus and Achilles is explained by both being connected to the belief in life after death.

Likewise, Rudston's singular Venus and *bestiarii* (hunters) mosaic with its North African allusions such as the crescent topped staff, the symbol of the Telegenii, is possibly third century and the product of a local workshop adapting an imported design. The Telegenii were a professional guild of hunters whose patron deity was Bacchus and who supplied beasts for the arena hunts. Iconographically they are widely attested in North Africa. The figures are heavily coloured and the shock-haired male and female hunters reminiscent of the barbarians seen on North African mosaics. The central 'pool' panel is surely visually abbreviated from a design featuring a seated goddess in a shell accompanied by tritons and with Cupid holding her mirror. Two of its four animals are identified by inscriptions as occurs on North African mosaics portraying arena *venationes* (wild beast hunts);

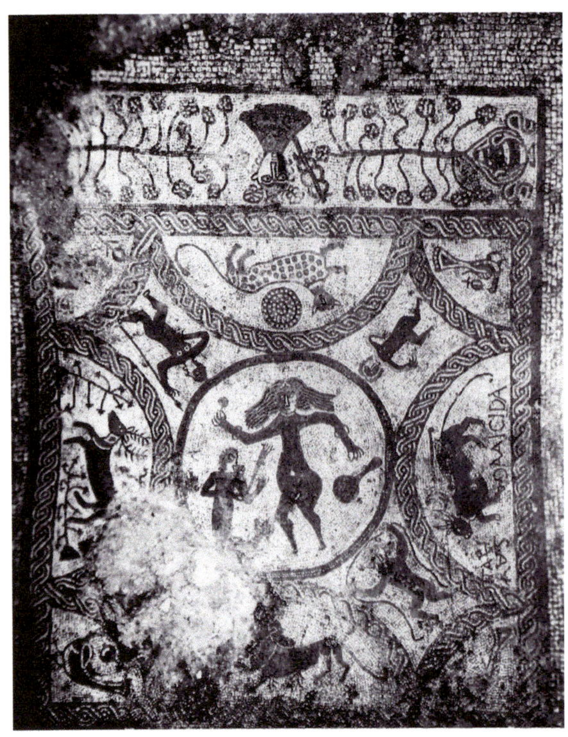

Left: A 1933 overhead excavation photograph of the Rudston Venus mosaic, now in the splendid mosaic collection at Hull and East Riding Museum. (Author's collection)

Below: Fragments of London's Birchin Lane mosaic as found in June 1857. The sea beast is in the Museum of London's collection but the apse fragment has been forgotten by academic writers and appears here for the first time since 1857. (Author's collection)

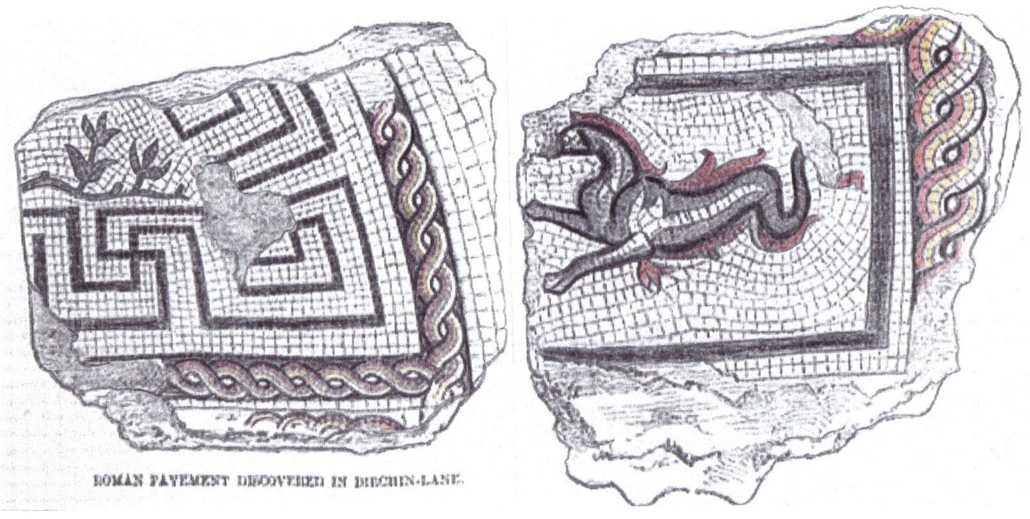

the speared lion as 'LEO FLAMMEFER' (fiery lion) and the bull as 'TAURUS OMICIDA' (man-killing bull). A leopard accompanied by a circular shield may refer to one of the methods of capturing the beast where hunters with shields surround and crowd the animals into transportation crates. Flanking side panels feature strange *canthari* from which grow flowering plants seen as grapes by some. A central bust of Mercury with a winged cap and caduceus is sometimes described as Bacchus with grapes in his hair and holding a *thyrsus*. However, even an illiterate mosaicist would surely know the difference between the attributes of two of Britain's most popular deities. The other damaged flowery side panel may have featured Bacchus.

Some mosaics currently dated to the previous century may be later than assumed and others among the mass assigned to the fourth century pushed back at least to the late third. London also has mosaics of this period. Birchin Lane's mosaic fragments featured a sea beast and an unusual guilloche-bordered apse containing a run of swastika-meander that has remarkably been forgotten by previous commentators. A leafy branch survived in its narrow lunette panel that possibly emanated from a *cantharus* as in the apse at Oulston, Yorkshire. Possibly its mosaicists also worked on a fine swastika-meander mosaic at Arthur Street. Bacchus on a tiger from Leadenhall Street, with its lavish use of glass tesserae, is believed to be mid-third century and the product perhaps of imported German mosaicists. The pelta and lozenge device in its borders and use of glass tesserae are features of mosaics from Trier. Its mosaicists are tentatively credited with two Verulamium mosaics and other London pavements that feature a distinctive acanthus flower such as Bucklersbury's. The firm has been named the 'Londinian Acanthus Group'. Bignor's superb figured mosaics, which bear comparison with some in Gaul, and may be judged as technically the finest in Britain, possibly date from the late third century and be the work of an imported mosaicist. Their quality shows that technical brilliance was still available and acquired through continual patronage of the artform.

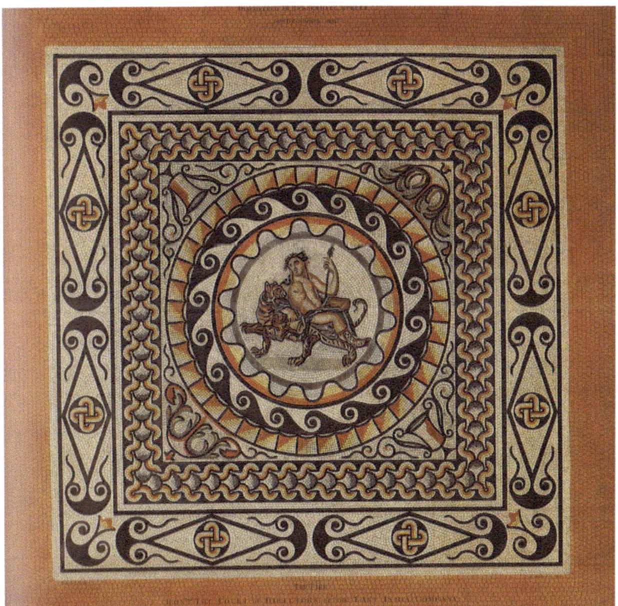
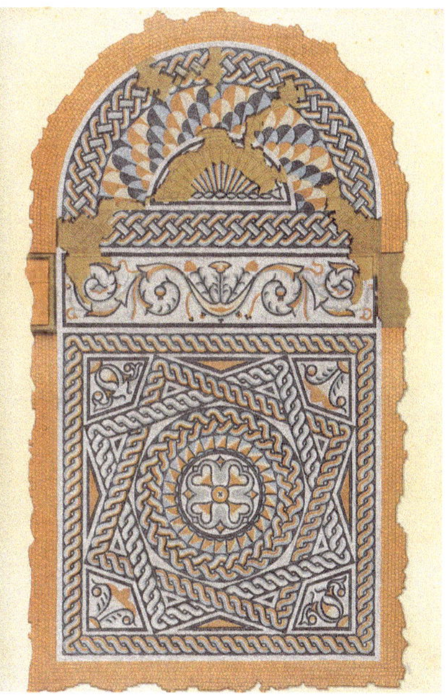

Above left: Bacchus on a tiger from Leadenhall Street, London, found in 1803 and possibly the work of third-century mosaicists from Trier. Fragments in the British Museum. 1804 engraving by J. Roffe. (Author's collection)

Above right: The third-century Bucklebury mosaic, now in the Museum of London, was excavated in 1869. Ascribed to the Londinian Acanthus firm through its distinctive acanthus flowers, it features an early use of interlaced squares. Lithograph by R. Canton. (Author's collection)

10

Fourth-Century Resurgence

The apparent slump in mosaic laying was remarkably reversed at the end of the third century both in town and countryside. The reason for this resurgence is still debated and was once put down to the flight of capital from provinces menaced by barbarian incursions. Britain had been divided into four provinces around AD 296, and Britannia Prima, centred on Cirencester, was paramount with its wealth possibly based on wool. British villas were expanded, many reaching new heights of architectural sophistication. This was the golden age for mosaics throughout Britain and especially in the south and west. There must have been many firms as well as jobbing mosaicists in existence throughout this century, and they were no doubt peripatetic in seeking commissions. There appears to have been some cooperation on large commissions and possibly figure mosaicists may have moved between firms where required. Mosaicists from the south-west (where schemes incorporating interlaced squares became particularly popular) now appear to have been called upon to provide mosaics for clients in London and the south-east. There seem to be relatively few

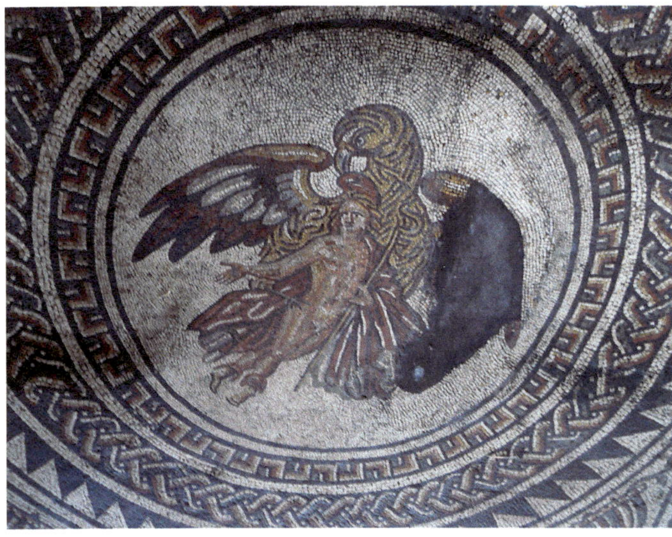

The Rape of Ganymede by Jupiter as an eagle encapsulates the superb quality of Bignor villa's late third-century figured mosaics that are the finest in Britain and still in situ. (Robert Field)

fourth-century mosaics in the south-east and none that can be grouped to form a firm's oeuvre, but this may be through chance of survival or that sites remain unlocated.

David Smith's 'schools' (i.e. family firms) of mosaicists date from this century. He had originally linked and detected the mosaics of four important producers. Two he placed in Corinium. The first was responsible for mosaics at Woodchester, Chedworth, Stonesfield and Barton Farm. Their work is easily identified by its quality, distinctive acanthus scrolls and highly decorative figure work. They specialised in Orpheus pavements, their greatest commission being that at Woodchester. Their pavements are often bordered by an elegant meander pattern with inset panels of guilloche. An apparent offshoot of this firm is the Corinian Saltire Group, named after their prominent use of the saltire design in their mosaics. Their work (or influence) is found at such sites as Cirencester, North Leigh, Stonesfield and Chedworth. It has become apparent that attributions are far more complicated than was once imagined and a further offshoot, employing the saltire design, produced mosaics at Halstock, Lopen, Queen Camel and Broad Street, London, and is

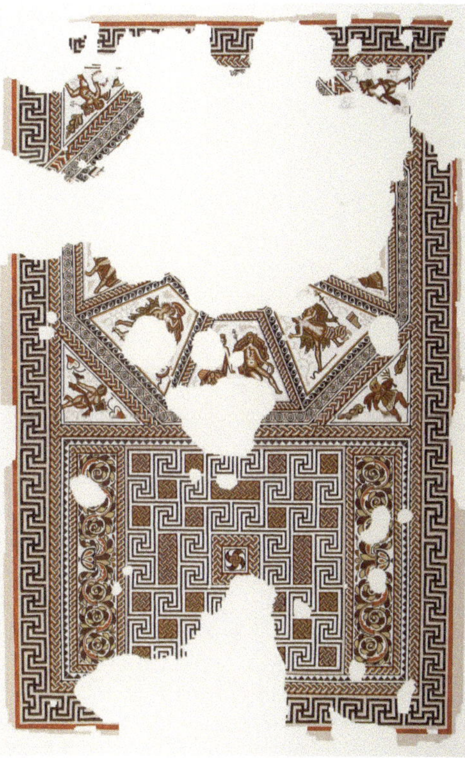

Above left: The Corinian Bacchus mosaic from Stonesfield, Oxfordshire, as recorded by Michael Burghers in 1712. Bacchus held a *thyrsus* and a *cantharus* and was accompanied by a leopard. (Author's collection)

Above right: Luigi Thompson's superb recording of Chedworth's Bacchic mosaic in Room 5. Three dining couches were probably spaced around the central square swastika-pelta panel. An octagonal fountain pool probably filled the centre of the Bacchic octagon as at Woodchester. (Courtesy of Luigi Thompson)

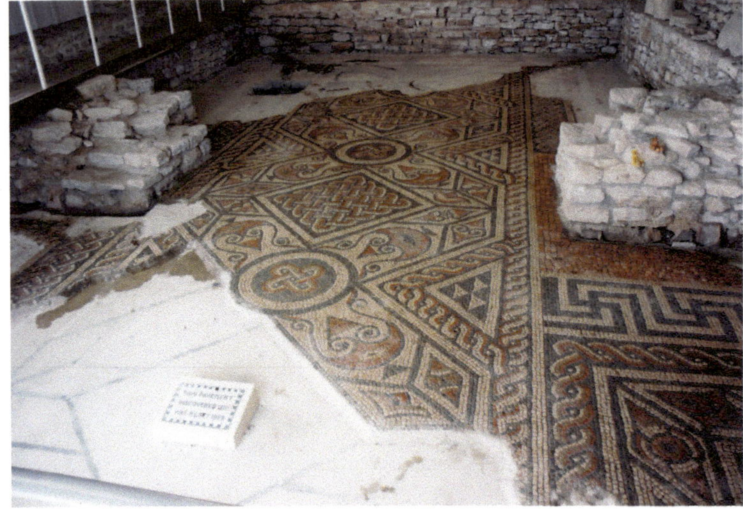

North Leigh's mosaic by the Corinian Saltire firm in Room 1. The entrance at the near left faced an alcove probably designed for holding a side table displaying silverware. (Author's photograph)

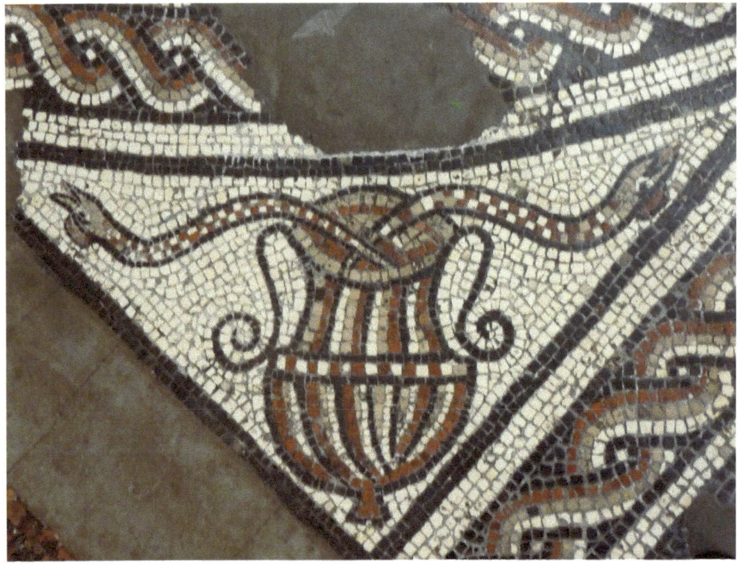

Crested and speckled agathodaemon serpents, bringers of prosperity and good fortune to a household, slither from a *cantharus* on the Durngate mosaic in the Dorset County Museum, Dorchester. (Author's photograph)

believed to have been based at Lindinis (Ilchester). Further related designs were being produced in areas around Gloucester and north along the Severn to Hereford, Shropshire, Worcestershire and South Wales.

The Durnovarian Group based around Durnovaria (Dorchester) or Ilchester are notable for their figured mosaics, found in south-western villas. Only the Durngate Street mosaic can be attributed them to in Dorchester itself. Evidently more than one figure worker was employed on their commissions as certain idiosyncrasies such as concertina-like muscles on animals' forelimbs, cleft chins and windswept hair seen on mosaics at Frampton and Hinton St Mary do not appear on all their attributed pavements if these indeed are actually their work at all. The Dewlish Leopard and Gazelle, saved for the nation in 2021 and now in

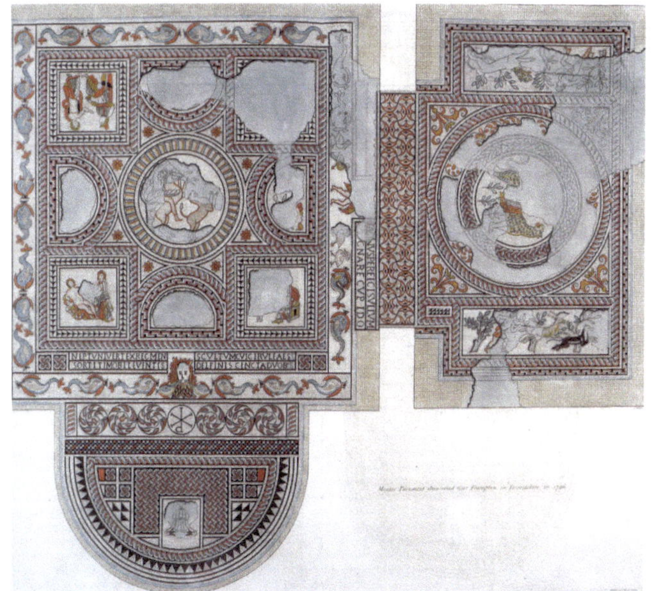

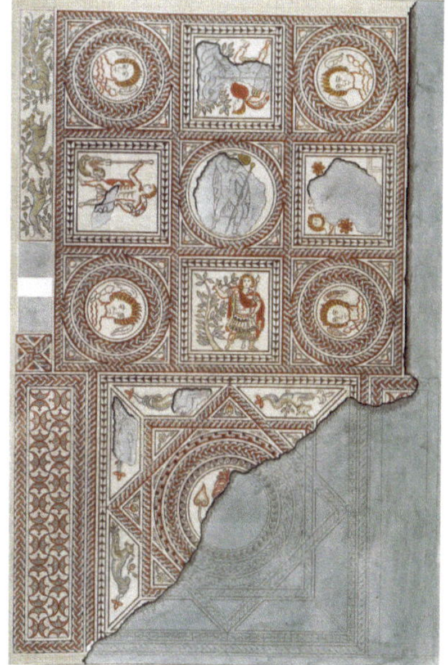

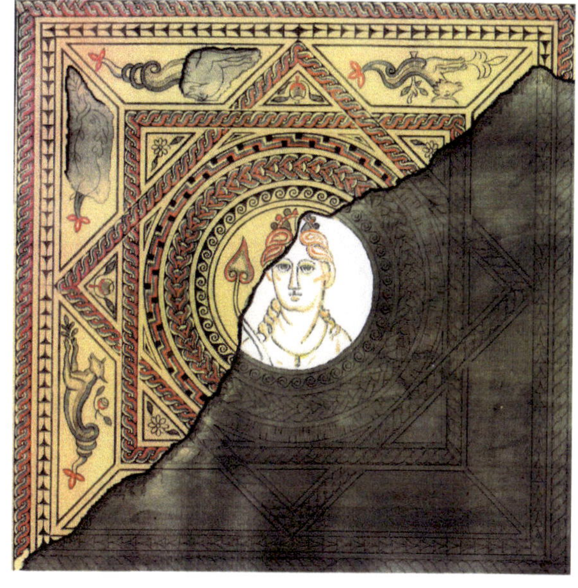

Above left: Frampton's Neptune and Cupid mosaic features a central Bellerophon roundel, panels referring to Venus, Bacchus on a leopard and a stylised pool in an apse. Lysons' recording. (Author's collection)

Above right: Frampton's Venus and the Winds mosaic. Panels feature Æneas and the Golden Bough, Neptune creating Scyphius from a stone and Cadmus and the serpent. Bacchus fills the central panel. Lysons' recording.(Author's collection)

Right: Author's restoration of Frampton's Venus panel restored in the cleft chin manner of the Durnovarian mosaicists. (Author's collection)

Dorchester museum, was either the work of a travelling master figurative mosaicist working with lesser local mosaicists or a bought in panel. It is also difficult to link the mosaics at Hemsworth and Fifehead Neville to their oeuvre. The discovery of the new 'Venus' mosaic at Bratton Seymour with its similar foliage to Fifehead Neville and its connections to Bratton's Diana pavement and others at Yatton and Bromham suggest either an offshoot or a separate firm. Likewise Low Ham's Æneas mosaic and that of Pitney may have more in common with each other than other figured mosaics of the Durnovarian Group.

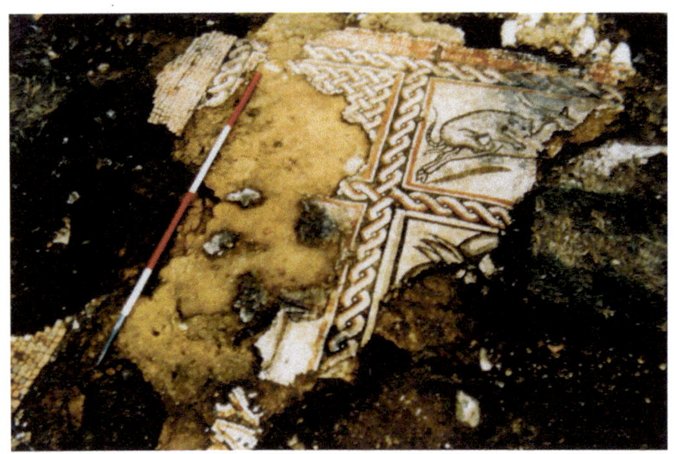

A surviving corner of Dewlish's hunting mosaic of Room 1. The quality of the panels suggests that either they were prefabricated or were done by a visiting master mosaicist. Four fish-legged tritons with seaweed aprons occupied corners and held up the central panel. (Bill Putnam collection, currently at Bournemouth University)

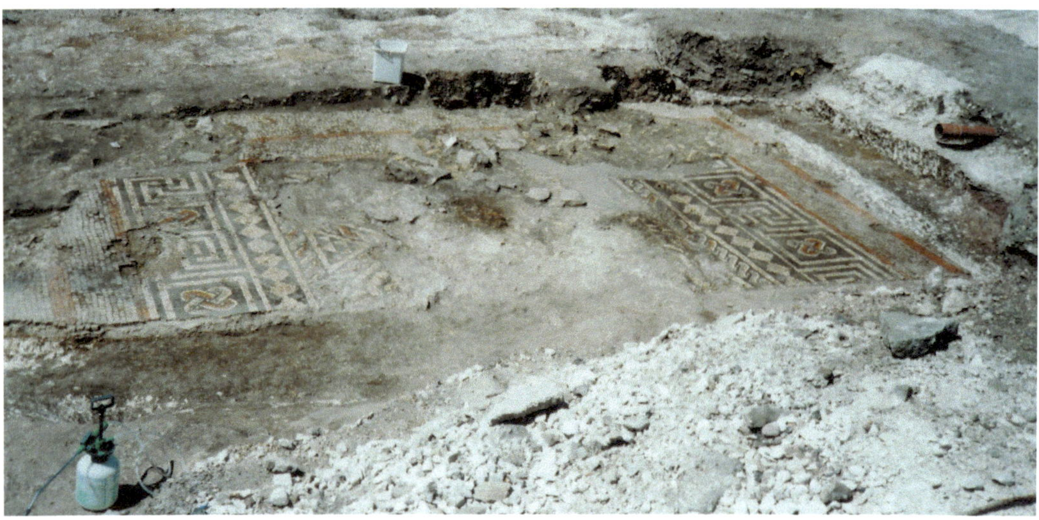

A beautiful fourth-century mosaic from Somerleigh Court, Dorchester, retained an exceptionally smooth finish and may be by the same mosaicists employed at the town's Colliton Park house. (David Ashford)

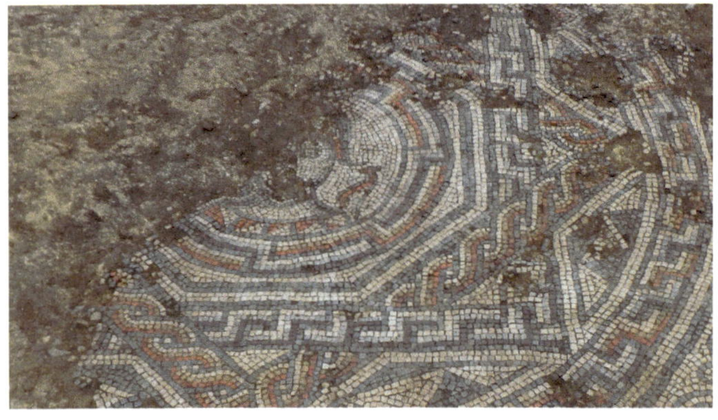

Bratton Seymour's Diana mosaic. She wears a *stephane* (diadem) and the end of a Scythian bow appears over her shoulder. Grey tesserae suggest a quiver rested on the other. (Author's collection)

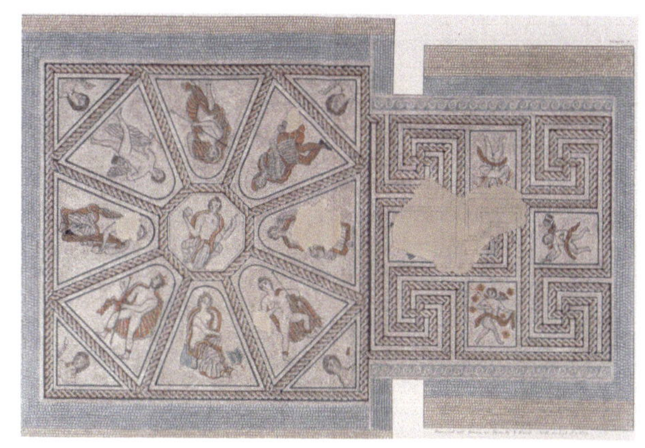

The mosaic from Pitney recorded by Samuel Hasell's lithograph. Bacchus and other figures appear to have upstanding hair possibly linking the mosaic to Frampton's Neptune and the Winds mosaicist. (Author's collection)

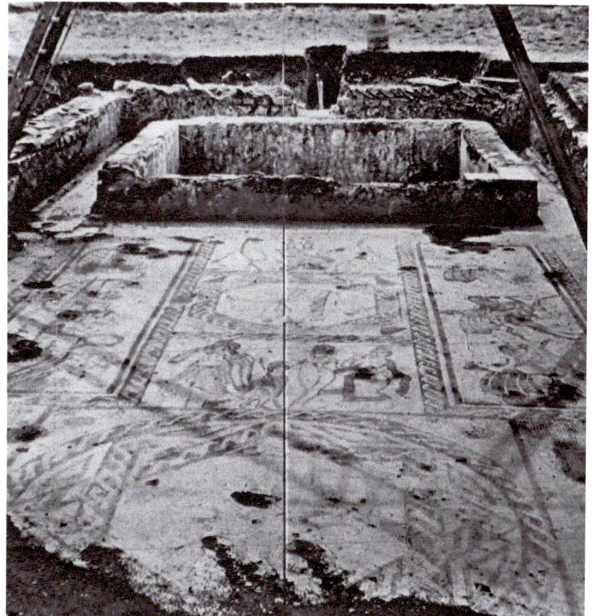

The Æneas mosaic, Low Ham, Somerset. A photograph taken at the 1946 excavation showing its original frigidarium setting with an impressive walled pool. (Author's collection)

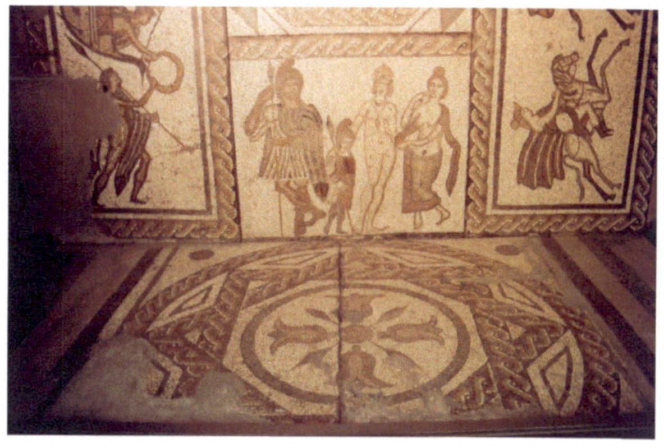

Low Ham's mosaic as once displayed in the Somerset County Museum, Taunton. The entrance panel is unfortunately no longer displayed. (Author's photograph)

Although the figure work of several mosaicists is recognisable, it is generally the geometric motifs and borders used that link a mosaic to a particular firm. Stephen Cosh has suggested a 'South-Western Group' producing mosaics at such sites as Keynsham, Box, Bradford on Avon and Holcombe. He also suggests that a similar firm was operating in the area around and beyond Bath that he terms the Southern Dobunnic Group that may have been responsible for mosaics at Littlecote and Wellow. Cosh has also proposed the Lindinis Group operating around Ilchester and notable for schemes using four pairs of interlaced squares as well as offshoots from the Corinium Saltire firm's designs. White borders with red lines on some of their mosaics suggest a link with examples at some south Dorset sites like Preston.

Following his excavation of Sparsholt's mosaic, David Johnston detected an additional firm that he named the Central Southern Group. Its mosaics are found mainly in Hampshire, Wiltshire and West Sussex. Largely geometric and employing interlaced squares, often within poised octagons, their attractive mosaics include Downton's,

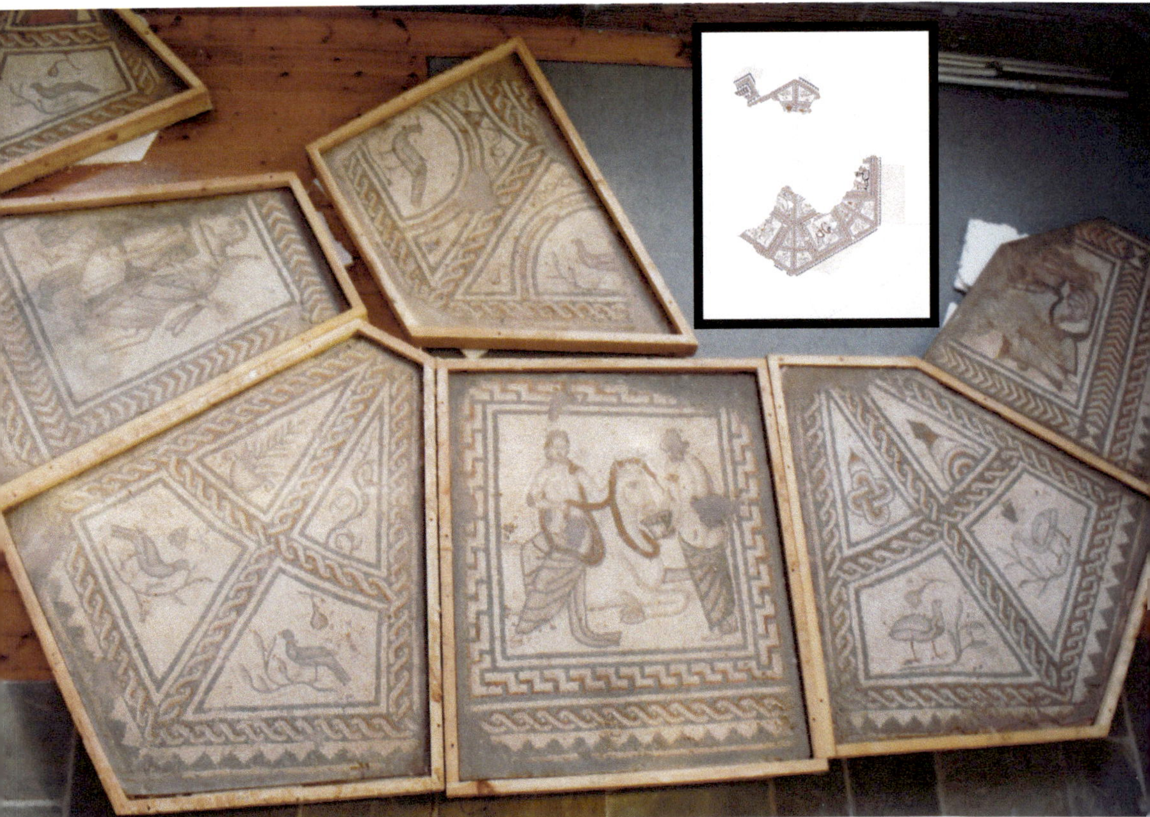

Mythological panels from Keynsham's Room W include Achilles on Skyros, Europa and the bull and Minerva and the invention of the double flute. Now under glass in the floor of Keynsham Library. (Author's photograph)

Inset: Stephen Cosh's recording of Room W. (Copyright Stephen Cosh)

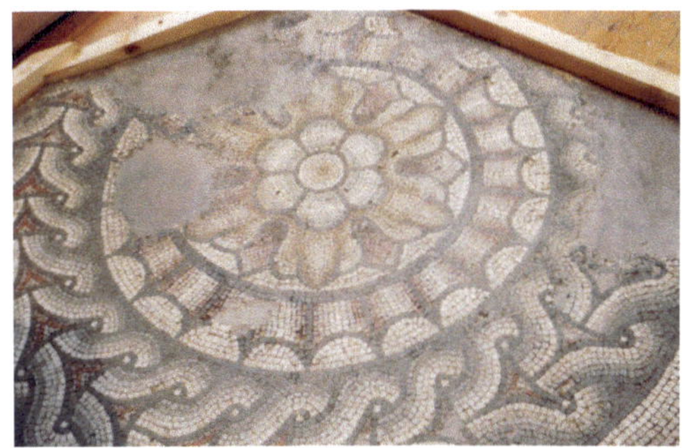

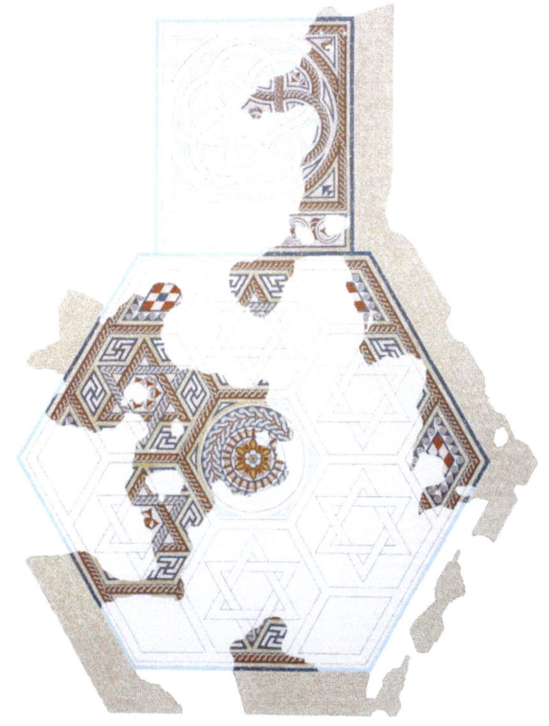

Above: The floral centrepiece of Keynsham's Room J is exceptionally fine in its sensitive handling of colour and is one of the finest examples of Romano-British mosaic. Now displayed in Keynsham Library. (Author's photograph)

Right: Stephen Cosh's watercolour recording of rooms J and K at Keynsham, which formed a spectacular centre to Britannia's most architecturally elaborate suite of chambers. (Copyright Stephen Cosh)

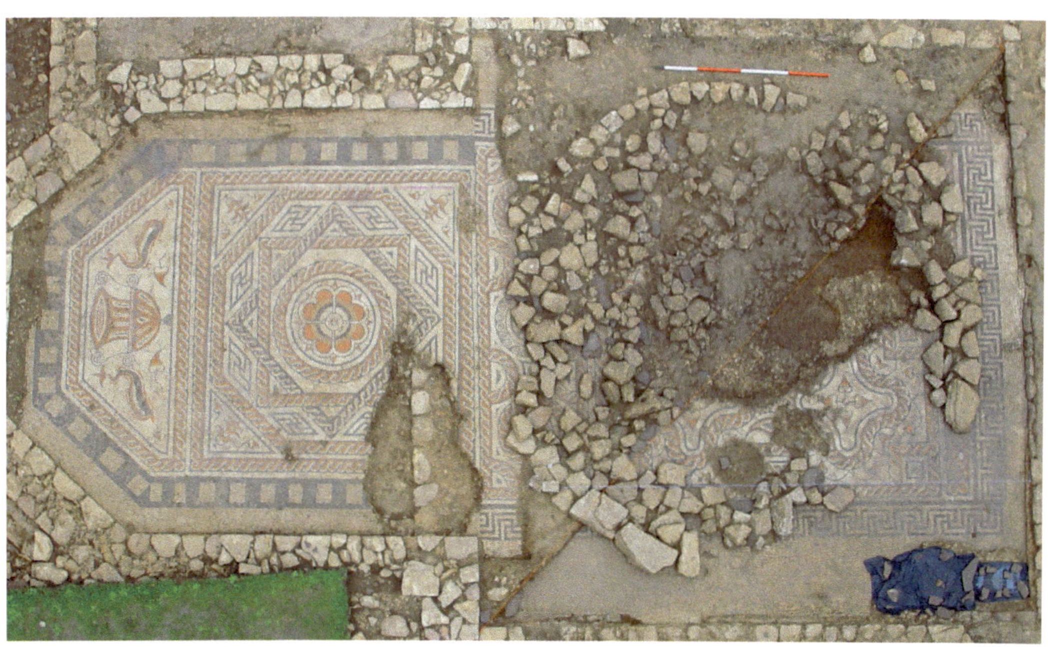

Bradford on Avon's villa mosaic featured an apse with a symbolic pool, interlaced squares with a lotus-flower centre and a lotus pool, similar to Brislington's with cushion-shaped islands, later covered by a baptistery. (Courtesy of Mark Corney)

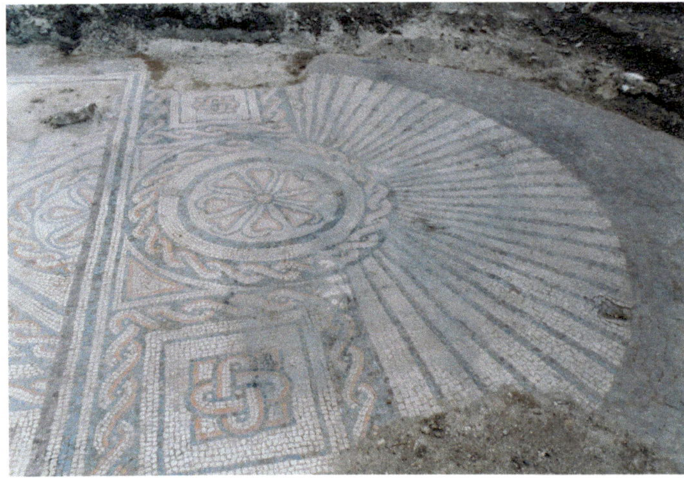

Badminton villa, Gloucestershire, has a remarkable mosaic featuring unique geometry and motifs (such as this floral rosette) by an innovative mosaicist. (Author's photograph)

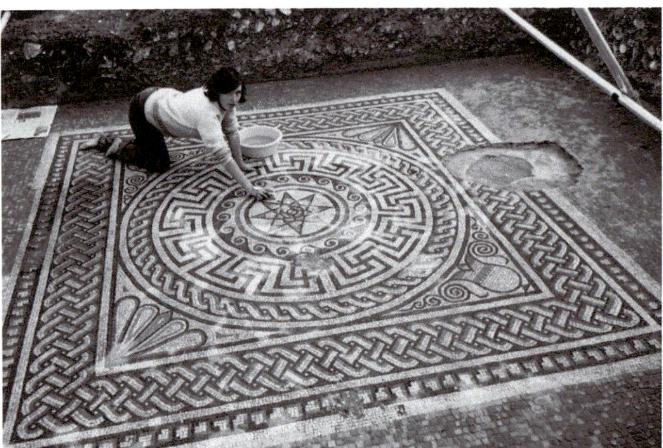

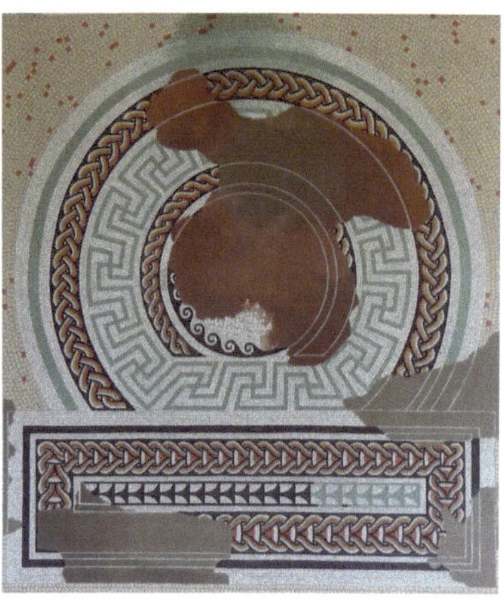

Above left: Sparsholt's mosaic being cleaned by June Wilbur of the Hampshire Field Club on 28 August 1968. (Author's collection)

Above right: A Central Southern Group mosaic from a *stibadium* apse in House 1, Insula XXVII, Silchester, as recorded by George Fox in *Archaeologia* 58, pt 1, 1902, 21–22, Plt 2., and now in Reading museum.

Chilgrove's and possibly Grateley's. Their use of the swastika-meander at Sparsholt and on the fine *stibadium* apse at House 1, Insula XXVII, Silchester, is particularly striking. Tri-panelled schemes as at West Meon and Itchen Abbas are a speciality. Bramdean's Hercules and Deities of the Week mosaics are credited to them with the assistance of a peripatetic figure mosaicist.

The situation in the North and Midlands is equally complicated. A Northern Group has been proposed that produced fine mosaics at Isurium (Aldborough) and sites in Yorkshire and Lincolnshire such as Beadlam, Malton, Winterton, Brantingham and Lincoln Castle. Designs often feature two rectangular side panels flanking a central square panel and may

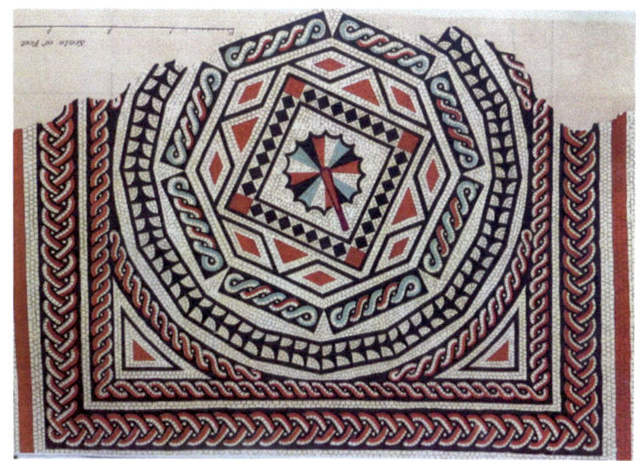

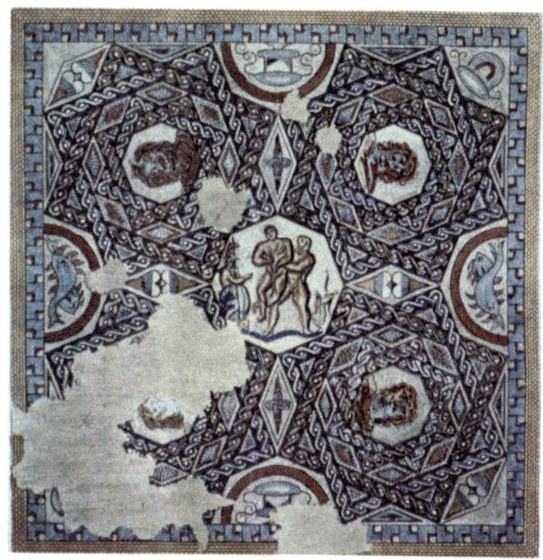

Above left: Grateley, Hampshire. The cockade fan mosaic is probably by the Central Southern Group of mosaicists and displays the commonest type of Roman fan. (Author's collection)

Above right: Bramdean. Hercules killing Antæus by lifting him away from his mother, the earth goddess Tellus, from whom he got his strength. Seasons fill the double interlaced squares, a scheme only known on one other British mosaic. Jacob and Johnson, 1839. (Author's collection)

Right: David Neal's recording of the Muses Mosaic from Brantingham. (Courtesy and copyright of David S. Neal)

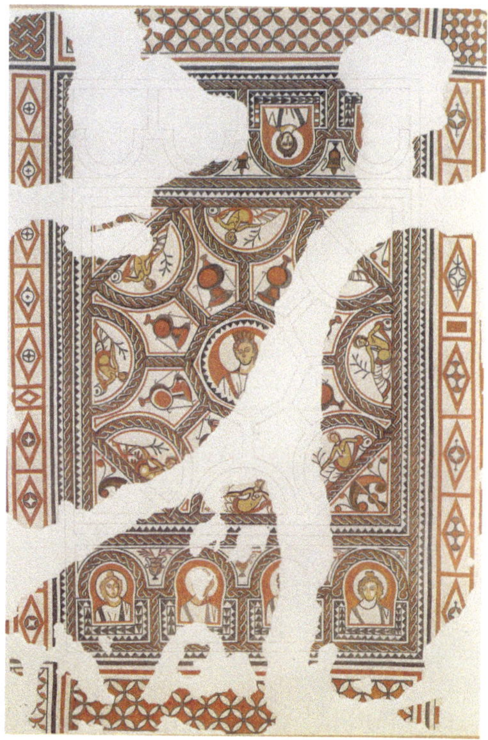

feature stepped triangles and large lozenges in the borders as at Winterton. Lozenges seem particularly popular in Aldborough together with sophisticated figured mosaics.

Mosaics attributed to the Midland Group of mosaicists occur at such places as Castor, Denton, Thistleton, Mansfield Woodhouse, Scampton and Stanwick. Durobrivae (Water Newton) or Leicester may have been their base. Their output appears wholly geometric beyond the occasional *cantharus*. Indeed the virtual absence of any figured work in the Midlands suggests a regional preference for geometric floors even though wall paintings feature figurative subjects. Schemes are based on squares separated by small poised squares with interspaces filled by eight-lozenge-stars. Often simple designs based on octagons or intersecting circles are found. Cosh and Neal have suggested the Midland Group mosaicists assisted on some of the Corinium Orpheus Group's geometric panels like Woodchester or Barton Farm.

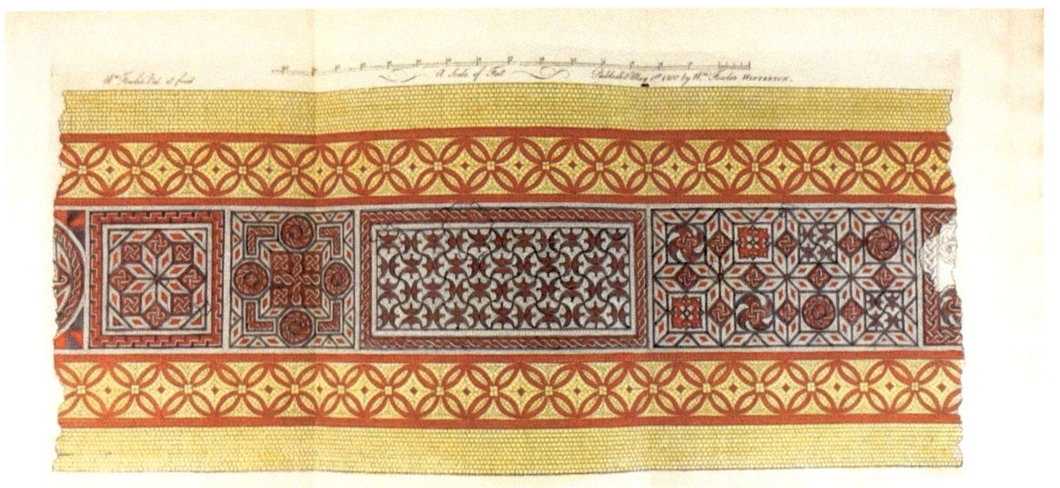

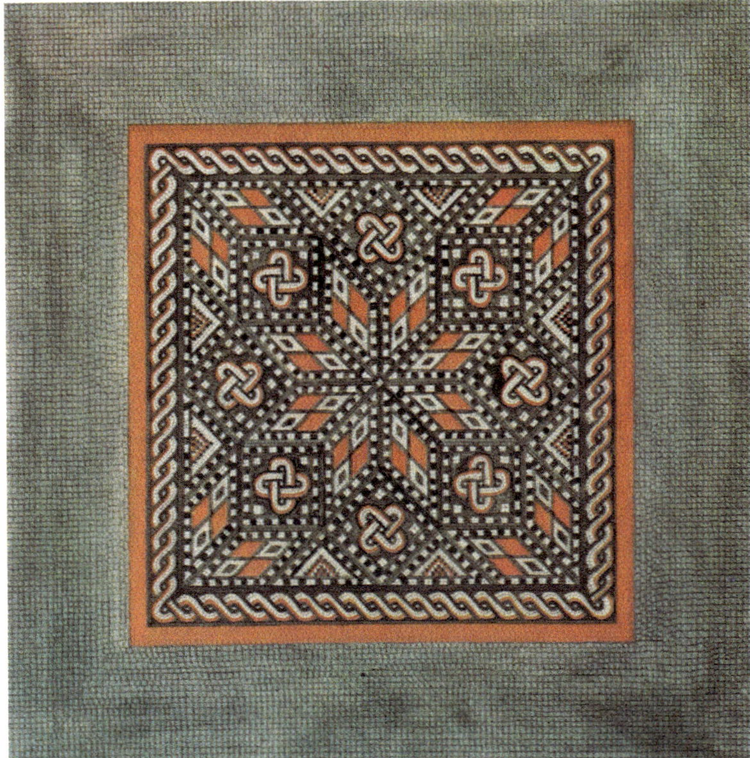

Above: William Fowler's engraving of the spectacular porticus mosaic from Scampton villa (Lincolnshire) that is credited to the Midlands Group of mosaicists. (Author's collection)

Left: A mosaic from Denton villa in Lincolnshire attributed to the Midlands Group as recorded by William Fowler. (Author's collection)

11

Fifth-Century Mosaics

Received academic knowledge always deemed the laying of mosaics after AD 410, the so-called 'end' of Roman Britain, to be improbable. This has seriously curtailed the dating that archaeologists have dared to give to mosaic and other artistic Romano-British discoveries. It has never seemed sensible to believe that civilised life suddenly ceased in Britannia and excavations in 2017 below the west wall of Room 28 at Chedworth villa uncovered charcoal, radiocarbon dated to AD 424–544, suggesting that the room and its mosaic were newly constructed well into the fifth century. Radiocarbon-dated bone and late pottery, including North African redware and a fragment of a sixth-century Palestinian amphora, support the continuation of civilised life there. The attractive mosaic with a border of open guilloche echoes that from the cella of the temple of Nodens at Lydney that overlay and post-dated a coin of Gratian of the 380s. Other possible late fourth- or fifth-century mosaics have been found at Cirencester, Ilchester Mead and Hucclecote, where the mosaic covered a coin of AD 395. Boxford's unique mosaic, incorporating artistic trends found in fifth-century ivory diptych carving and illumination, may itself date from that century.

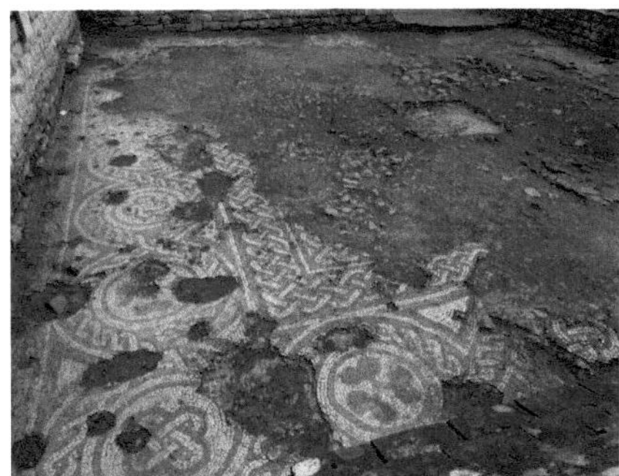
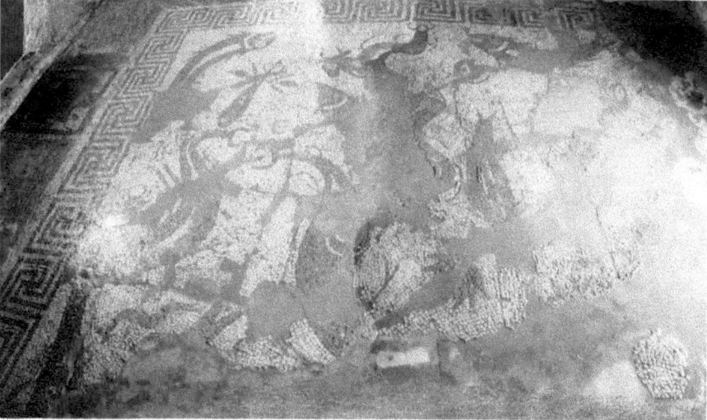

Above left: Radiocarbon dating suggests that the mosaic in Chedworth's Room 28 was laid after AD 424. Its attractive border design of open guilloche holds panels of confronted lotus leaves and knots. The room was still in use as a work hall in the fourteenth century. (Author's photograph)

Above right: The Italianate black and white figure marine mosaic at Great Witcombe, Gloucestershire. (Author's photograph)

12

Marine Mosaics

Marine mosaics, covered with a scatter of sea denizens, both natural and mythological, are found throughout the empire. Although widespread in Britain, perhaps, by chance of survival, not as many remain as might be expected. A fragmentary first-century AD marine mosaic in the black figure style ornamented the *frigidarium* of the fortress baths at Chester. Creatures with sinuous tails are striped in white to impart a three-dimensional effect to them. Another early marine mosaic is suspected from Eccles villa in Kent. The second-century Italian-style mosaic in the *frigidarium* of the lower baths at Great Witcombe, Gloucestershire, is the most extant. Since Charles Stothard's 1818 recording, about a quarter has since been lost through subsidence, although the author discovered one fragment in English Heritage's store. This charming riot of creatures is depicted in the black figure tradition with white body detailing and red fins. On some fish, white side flashes are intended to show shine and curvature. Creatures depicted include dolphins, rays, crabs and a flying fish with elaborate whirligig 'wings'. Three bivalves with siphon tubes appear, although Stothard omitted one which no commentator has noticed. Mythological creatures include a *hippocampus* (sea horse),

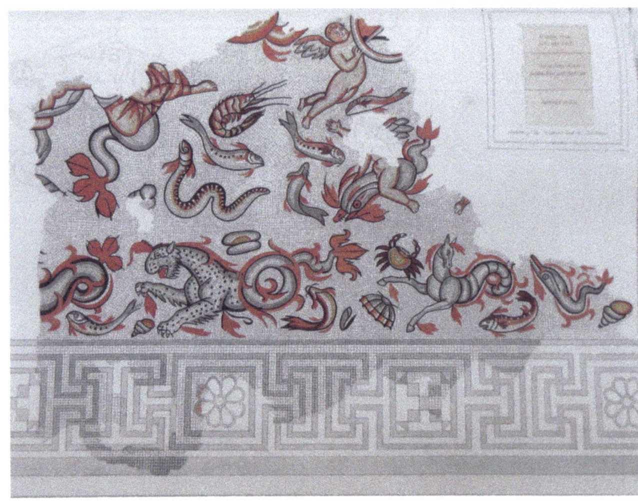

Cirencester's second-century Triumph of Neptune mosaic from Dyer Street, recorded by Lysons, is the finest known marine mosaic in Britain. (Author's collection)

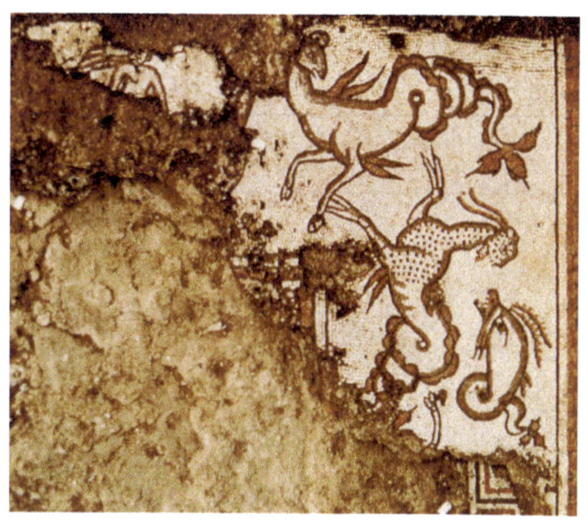

The Dewlish marine mosaic now in the Dorset Museum, Dorchester, featured a bad tempered dolphin and an *amorino* who was seemingly not lifted. (Bill Putnam Collection, currently at Bournemouth University)

bovicampus (sea bull) and a *capricornus* (sea goat). Possibly the long-necked, wolf-headed, plesiosaur-like *pistrix* occupied the centre. The cella mosaic from Lydney's temple of Nodens featured confronted *pistrices* and a *pistrix* also occurs at Kingscote.

Another second-century black figure pavement with entwined sea beasts and a bivalve was found at Llanfrynach, 70 miles away, in 1783. It survives in two recordings but perhaps half was already lost. Again the creatures have side stripes.

The most elaborate marine mosaic, dating from the second century, is the Triumph of Neptune from Dyer Street, Cirencester. Now buried, Samuel Lysons made two recordings of it and another slightly varying painting survives in the Wollaston Collection at the National Art Library. The mosaic featured the usual sea denizens including a *pardalocampus* (sea leopard/ panther) and *amorini* (cupids), one riding on a dolphin and another holding on to Neptune's chariot. A nereid rides on the tail of another beast or a triton. The animals are elaborately treated with grey three-dimensional shading and red fins. Some echoes of this mosaic appear in the elegant, and possibly second-century, Blue Coat School mosaic from Bath, now in the Roman Baths Museum. The placement of its surviving grey-shaded beasts suggests they come from a corner of the design. Toft Green, York, yielded a beautiful *bovicampus* from a marine mosaic that may have paved the baths of the Severan Imperial Palace.

At Bromham, Wiltshire, the marine mosaic was truncated by a later geometric mosaic. Its elegant but simple line-drawn inhabitants included several lotus leaves. A fine mid-fourth-century Durnovarian mosaic from Dewlish featured an irritable dolphin threatening a *pardalocampus*. An *amorino* seems to have been riding another sea beast or triton nearby. A framed central panel perhaps held the head of Neptune or a *cantharus* fountain. Concentric circles of fish and dolphins encircled a *cantharus* at Fifehead Neville. Neptune/Oceanus's bust often appears on foreign mosaics in the centre of a marine scatter as he does at Rudston surrounded by a border of lotus blossoms.

Marine creatures appear in the panels of many mosaics, either as references to that pavement's main subject or as a suitable supporting decoration. A mosaic from Caerwent featured an elaborate scheme of octagons each containing two fishes. Symbolic pool and water garden mosaics with marine denizens could ornament any room but naturally fish were most pertinent in bath suites such as at Lufton where they decorate the ambulatory surrounding the plunge bath.

13

Gardens, Symbolic Pools and Mosaics

A direct correlation existed between the geometric designs used for mosaics and those used for island water gardens and flower beds in the Roman world. Sometimes entire mosaics form symbolic water gardens or pools. One also finds the artistic convention prevalent in gardens of placing sculpture in front of trees (as found at Oplontis A and flanking the Canopus at Tivoli), replicated in mosaic where animals are backed by trees as at Horkstow and Winterton. Some mosaics are exact copies of garden designs while

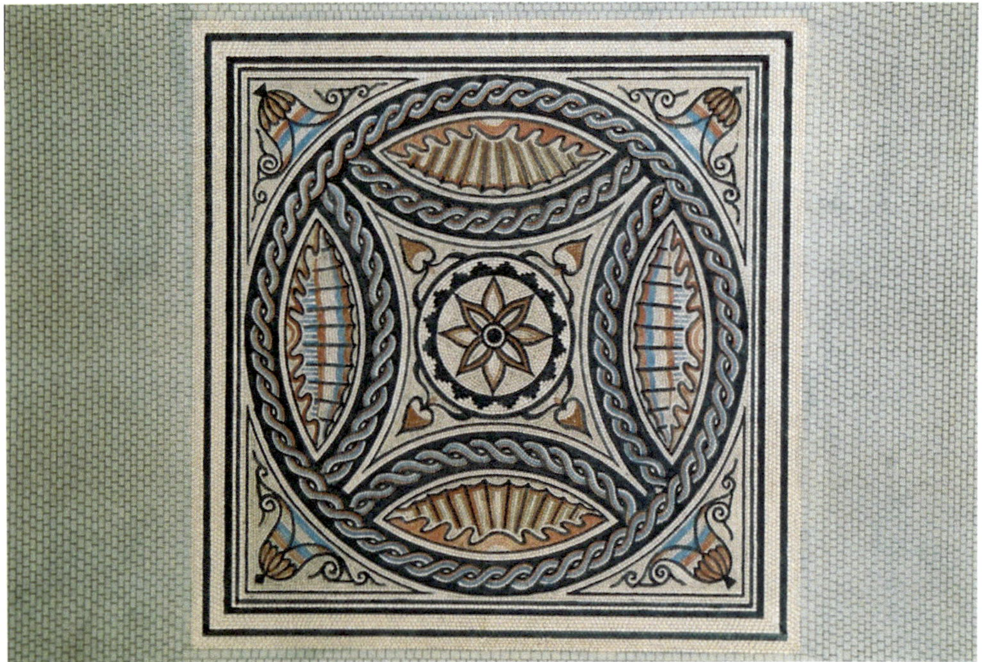

The Lea Cross mosaic as recorded by Thomas Telford in 1793 and copied in oilcloth for Matthew Boulton's Soho House. Scallop shells and lotus flowers the attributes of Venus. (Author's collection)

others only use elements. The indented or four-lunetted square of the Palatine's sunken garden and Conimbriga's water gardens in Portugal occurs widely in Britain and elsewhere. Indeed the complete Palatine design including its *pelta* islands is duplicated in a panel at the Marine Baths at Sabratha, Libya. At Olympia, the Leonidaion's cushion-shaped island in its peristyle water garden is found again adapted in British mosaics. A fourth-century mosaic from Brislington, Bristol, uses four cushion islands 'planted' with flowers and spaced around a central square island featuring a *cantharus*. The field surrounding the cushions features lotus while dolphins and other marine denizens fill compartments on each side. A similar mosaic 'pool' later covered with a Christian baptistery was found at Bradford on Avon.

Stylised mosaic representations of gardens, fountain pools and fishponds are symbolic of the desire for status achieved by the real thing. The lotus/waterlily was an extremely popular motif in Roman mosaic, but particularly on Romano-British mosaics. Its bud, leaf and flower appear everywhere. Its leaf is often confused with that of the ivy on mosaics as both are similar in Roman art. Venus' lotus symbolised rebirth, opening and closing with the day and born each spring from the mud. Such mosaics as that at the Verulamium Park hypocaust should be interpreted as resembling a lotus pool. The connection between mosaics and water gardens seems particularly strong in northern provinces where winter frosts made elaborate outside water features and fountains problematic. Symbolic mosaic water gardens and fountain depictions are often found, hence at Frampton, Kingscote and Hemsworth, Venus appears in symbolic pools accompanied by sea creatures or lotus flowers. At Woodchester, Orpheus charms adjacent to a central fountain pool once patterned with fish and encircled by animals and bay and acanthus 'hedges', beyond which water nymphs sport in their pools. This recalls such fountain-encircled, statue-filled garden beds as Pompeii's House of M. Lucretius. Many indented-square mosaics that feature sea creatures or lotus leaves in the lunettes should be viewed as water gardens.

Bignor, Woodchester and Chedworth's rooms 25b and probably 5 possessed real pools no doubt featuring *canthari* or other forms of fountains. The pierced socle of one survived at Great Witcombe. However, symbolic fountain pools occur throughout British mosaics either occupying central panels as on the fountain mosaics from Verulamium and Downton, Wiltshire, or as the central element in an apse at Bradford on Avon, or Frampton. At Whatley, garden urns in symbolic garden beds are spaced around an apse where a lunette decorated with a fish symbolises a pool. In the northern provinces, where frost made the provision of the external D-shaped nymphaeum pools problematic, one finds internal mosaic copies. In warmer climes these open pools were often lined with marine mosaics and improved the view into the garden from reception rooms. Although several are known in Britain, only one from Head Street, Colchester, is known to have had mosaic and that apparently was plain white and later replaced with plaster presumably after frost damage. Verulamium's famous second-century scallop/cockle shell mosaic was designed to be viewed from a reception room across a corridor in much the same way as a nymphaeum would be. The shell was Venus' symbol and a mosaic from Lea Cross, Shropshire, featured four in a unique and possibly third-century pool design. Within a circle four ellipses contain scallops around a circular field holding a lotus flower. This mosaic was drawn on discovery in 1793 by the engineer Thomas Telford, who was working on the Ellesmere canal. The author was delighted when visiting Soho House in Birmingham (once owned by Telford's friend Matthew Boulton) to see a reproduction oilcloth on the floor of its entrance hall featuring the mosaic. It had been restored for the house using a line drawing discovered in correspondence but without knowing its antiquity, and thus the colours are wrong and the design simplified. It was a delight to inform the museum of the history of their 'mosaic'. Boulton commissioned the original oilcloth in 1798/9 via his interior designer Cornelius Dixon from the makers, Smith and Baber of Knightsbridge. Thomas Downing painted it. The Lea Cross pavement is one of the most sophisticated Romano-British pavements. Its shells and lotus leaves are symbols of Venus, while the spandrels hold lotus urns. A related design survives on an early third-century mosaic from Trier.

A mosaic from Fifehead Neville, Dorset, by the same mosaicist responsible for the Hemsworth Venus, featured a central *cantharus* 'fountain' surrounded by concentric circles in the manner of an Orpheus design. The first contained fish, the second the same three-dimensional finless dolphins as at Hemsworth. Other mosaics at Kingscote and Fordington High Street, Dorchester, depict deities such as Venus and Neptune emerging from their 'waters'. At Littlecote the mosaicist used a symbolic zig-zag water pattern, much used on the Continent but almost unique in Britain, to represent a rectangular pool as a threshold to the triconchial chamber.

In Mediterranean provinces floral mosaic borders occasionally ornamented the edges of flower beds, and courtyard mosaics incorporated keyhole plantings within their surface so that art was juxtaposed with nature in much the same way that garden walls were painted with a backdrop of dense foliage and birdlife. If such mosaics were ever in Britain they have not survived.

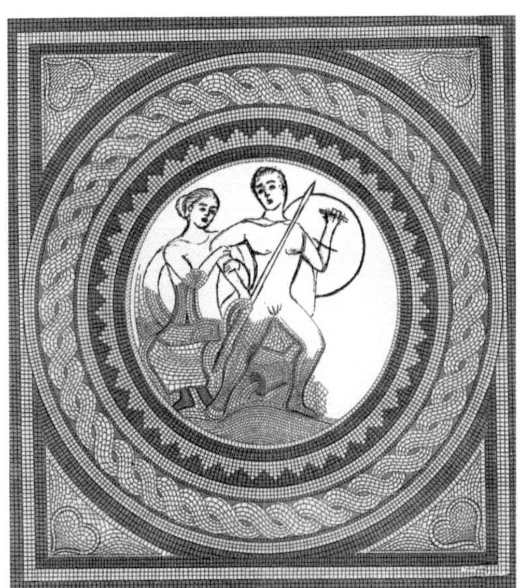
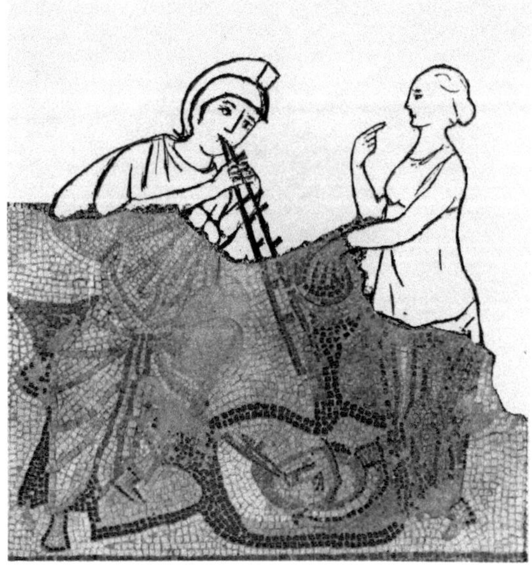

Two mosaics that drew on paintings by Famulus, of which there were copies in Nero's Golden House in Rome. A lost mosaic from Rudge depicting Achilles on Skyros restrained by Deidamea, and Keynsham's Minerva discovering that playing the flute distorts her face. Famulus' painting introduced the pose of Minerva's raised foot. (Author's reconstructions)

14

Myths and Mosaics: A Selection

Achilles

Achilles on Skyros was one romantic episode from the Greek hero's life widely reproduced on mosaics. To save him from his early death at Troy, Thetis hid him among the daughters of King Lycomedes dressed as a girl. He loved Princess Deidamea by whom some say he had a son. Desiring Achilles to join the Trojan expedition, Odysseus visited Skyros disguised as a peddler selling women's fripperies but included weapons among them. Arranging for a war trumpet to sound the alarm, the girls fled, but Achilles instantly took up shield and spear to fight and betrayed his identity. Mosaics at Keynsham, Rudge and Brading depicted this scene. That at Rudge copied the two central figures from the famous painting by Famulus in Rome's Golden House of Nero. The Achilles cycle on Horkstow's Medallions Mosaic includes it. In November 2021, a highly important late Roman Achilles mosaic with three scenes from Aeschylus' lost play, *Achilleis*, including the weighing of Hector's body for ransom (only known from one mosaic at Caddeddi, Sicily) was found in Rutland and again displays the culture of the owner.

Bacchus

The most popular deity on Romano-British mosaics is Bacchus, whom Greeks called Dionysos. Bacchus' *thiasus* (ecstatic retinue) includes Ariadne, Silenus, Pan, centaurs, bacchantes, satyrs and fauns. Allied to his *thiasus* are Priapus and Hercules. Ivy and grape vines represent him on mosaics as does the *cantharus* or wine cup. In British mosaic studies the difference between the *crater* (wine mixing bowl) and *cantharus* is blurred and most vessels are called 'a cantharus'. Theatrical masks, drum-like tambourines, *peda* (shepherd's crooks), panthers/leopards and tigers were Bacchic symbols or familiars. Panthers were good topers, drinking or heraldically flanking *canthari* as at Littlecote. Bacchus reclines or rides on a feline as at Leadenhall Street, London. Tigers refer to his triumphant return from India. The *thyrsus*, Bacchus' sacred staff, is carried by the god and his retinue. Sometimes ivy-topped or with a pinecone but occasionally by one or two short crossbars as at Brading or Pitney. These may be staffs of divinity, however, as other gods at Pitney hold them. Rurality, inebriated sexuality, and enjoyment imbued his entourage. The orgiastic dance of the bacchantes and satyrs added a lively aesthetic to his imagery. Silenus, his fat, balding companion reclines on an ass's back at Dyer Street, Cirencester. At Bignor ecstatic bacchantes whirl around a central pool where no doubt a *cantharus* fountain once played, and Jupiter abducts the beauteous Ganymedes to be his bedfellow and cupbearer in a reception room geared to hedonism. Chedworth's triclinium (Room 5) boasts an octagon of frenzied couplings overseen by Bacchus and Ariadne. The *peda* here echo the unusually shaped ones at Pitney. Bacchus discovering the deserted sleeping Ariadne on Naxos was a popular subject throughout the empire but only known in Britain from a drawing of a lost mosaic from East Coker, Somerset. He dominated a spectacular lost mosaic by the Corinian mosaicists at Stonesfield, Oxfordshire, discovered in 1712. The god's pre-Christian ability to turn water into wine and the mystery aspects of his cult that promised rebirth made his worship a rival to Christianity. His connection with the Orphic mysteries at Littlecote is evident in that mosaic's iconography. Bacchic imagery made an ideal decoration for dining and reception rooms as may be witnessed at Chedworth regardless of whether any deeper message was connected to the depictions.

Europa

Jupiter's abduction and rape of Princess Europa while in the form of a bull features on mosaics from Keynsham, Lullingstone and possibly on the mosaic from Old Broad Street, London.

Four Winds

Several mosaics feature the Venti or the Four Winds in corner panels. They again represent the seasons on a floor, with Favonius (Greek: Zephyros), the west wind and god of fructifying spring breezes, and Auster (Notos) the south wind god of summer rainstorms. Eurus (Euros), the east wind, must have represented autumn and Aquilo (Boreas) the north and the cold breath of winter. He is generally portrayed as bearded in most ancient representations but Romano-British winds are beardless. The Venti were popular with the Durnovarian and Lindinis mosaicists. Two mosaics at Frampton by different figure mosaicists feature them. One set adjacent to the Marine Venus mosaic displays the distinctive cleft chin and have head wings, whereas the set surrounding Neptune's bust are wingless and have gentler features. All carry long shell trumpets to blow. Others are known from Brading, Halstock, East Coker and Pitney, where Venus with a lotus leaf (fan?) substitutes for Favonius and spring. The Greeks originally only recognised three seasons or Horae and associated seasonal winds so possibly Pitney's mosaic enshrines this unless the goddess formed a repair. At Hinton St Mary, winds may have been customised to represent the Evangelists.

Ganymede

The abduction and rape of the Trojan Prince Ganymede by Jupiter in the form of an eagle appears at Bignor.

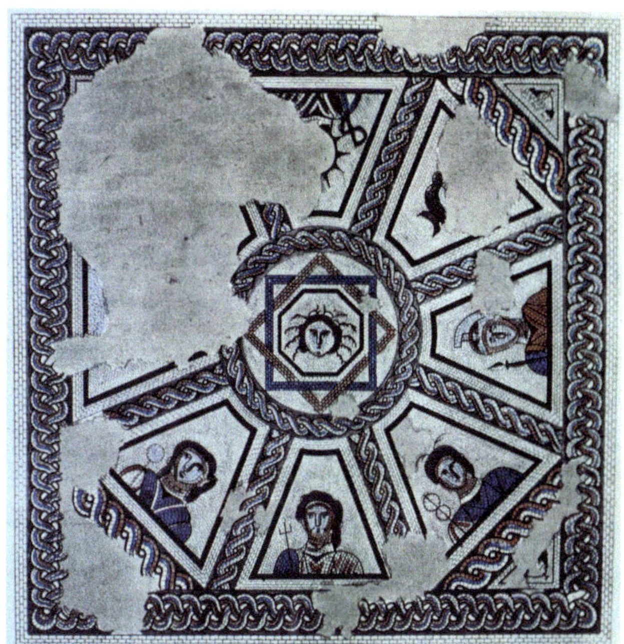

Deities of the week mosaic from Bramdean villa arranged clockwise with Sol (Sunday) and Luna (Monday) at the top. Engraving by Jacob and Johnson, 1839. (Author's collection)

Gods of the Week

The deities of the week appear with their attributes and are Sol/Sunday (whip and sun rays), Luna/Monday (crescent moon and whip or torch), Mars/Tuesday (helmet and spear), Mercury/Wednesday (caduceus and head wings), Jupiter/Thursday (thunderbolt, often with 'trident' ends), Venus/Friday (mirror, leaf fan and occasionally a peacock feather in North Africa, and possibly at Winterton, Lincolnshire) and Saturn/Saturday (a sickle). In the north-western provinces they feature on Jupiter columns as at Great Chesterford, Essex, and also on a castration clamp concerned with the worship of Cybele from London. Only one lost British mosaic from Bramdean, Hampshire, featured them with each deity filling a trapezoidal compartment within an octagonal design. Although damaged, only Saturn and the eighth compartment were fully lost. The extra compartment on Jupiter columns is often filled by Fortuna ('good fortune'), seemingly appropriate for a domestic setting, or Victoria (victory). The Cybele clamps add Ceres, goddess of agriculture to the assembly. The centre of the mosaic featured the head of Medusa as an apotropaic charm.

Hercules

Hercules appears on two British mosaics both featuring episodes connected to his Twelve Labours. At Bramdean his fight against Antæus, whom he could only kill by lifting him off the ground and crushing him, was depicted. At Boxford, he kills a centaur, either during the fight at Pholus' cave or his killing of Nessus for attempting to rape his wife. At Brading a damaged panel is purported to show his drinking contest with Bacchus.

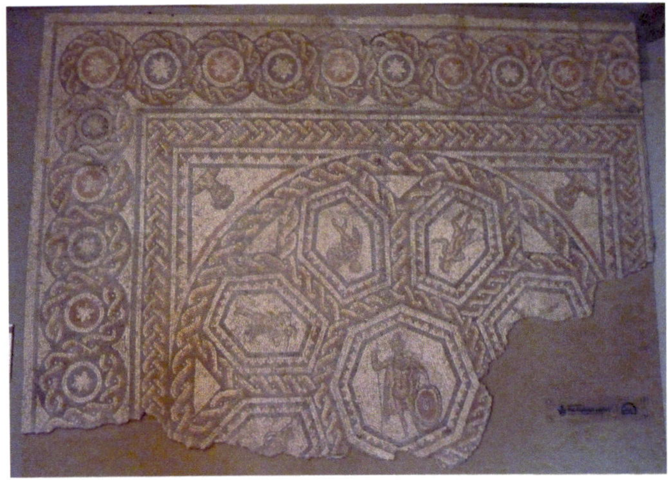

The Mars and satyrs
mosaic from Fullerton
now in Museum of
the Iron Age, Andover.
(Author's photograph)

Mars

Mars, god of war, was the paternal deity of Rome and a protector of crops and controller of wild places. In this guise he appears on the mosaic from Fullerton, surrounded by satyrs.

Medusa

The head of the gorgon Medusa (the *Gorgoneion*) appears widely in Roman art and frequently on mosaics as a central emblem. Its presence was apotropaic to the beholder and household and a guard against the evil eye. Originally portrayed in art as a terrifying creature, by Roman times she had become beautiful but with serpent hair and often sprouting wings at her temples. At Brading one of the mosaic panels there, based on classic paintings, depicts Perseus showing Andromeda the reflection of Medusa's head.

Minerva

The goddess appears on a panel from Keynsham relating the story of her invention of the double flute. Based on a painting by Famulus in Nero's Golden House, it depicts Minerva viewing her unfavourable reflection in a stream while blowing them. Its nymph points to her lips to emphasise the point, after which Minerva discarded the instrument.

Muses

The Nine Muses, inspirational goddesses of the arts and science, appear on at least two British mosaics. Aldborough's probably fourth-century mosaic was of exceptional sophistication, employing glass tesserae and Greek inscriptions. Its line of Muses

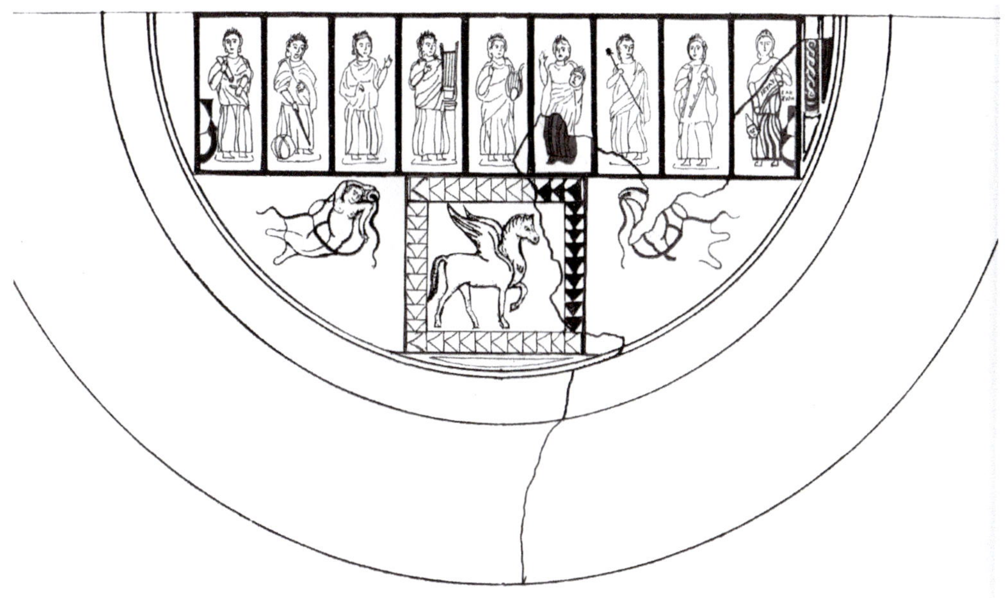

Above: Author's interpretative reconstruction to provide an idea of the original appearance of the Aldborough Muses mosaic based on H. E. Smith's engraving. It suggests an interpretation of Smith's rendering of one of two water nymphs, perhaps the Hippocrene and Aganippe, streams struck by Pegasus. (Author's collection)

Right: The surviving Muse and fragments in Aldborough site museum display the exceptional quality of the mosaic that employed glass tesserae. (Author's photograph)

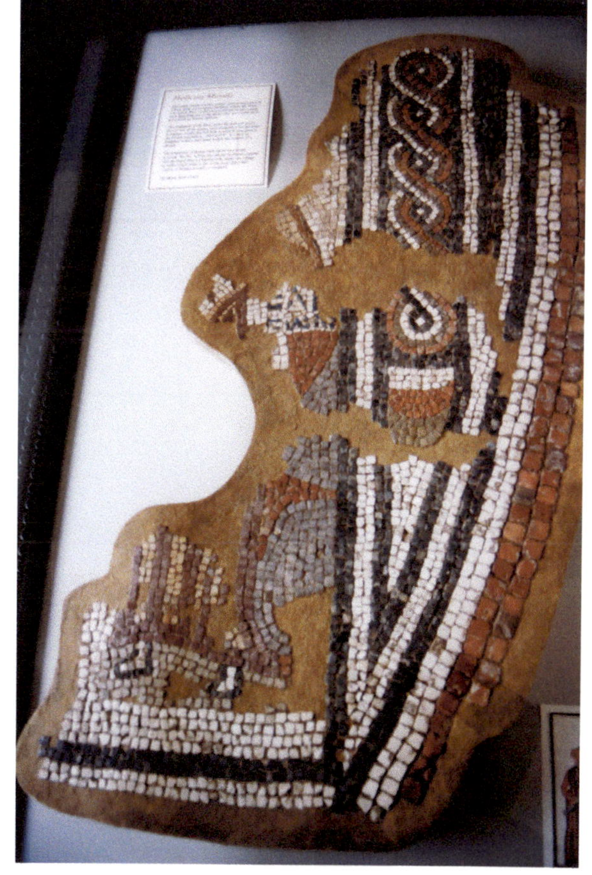

spanned an apsidal chamber. The surviving panel includes their home Mount Helicon that may have been symmetrically matched by a depiction of its location, Boeotia. The nymphs of Hippocrene and Aganippe (streams struck by Pegasus' hoofs) flanked a panel possibly showing Pegasus or perhaps Apollo, the Muses' patron. It may follow a formula found on a new mosaic from Antakya, Turkey, featuring the Muses, Helicon, Boeotia, the Hippocrene and the bathing of Pegasus by water nymphs. At Brantingham a central bust may wear the Muses' feathered crown while her sisters either recline as water nymphs in reference to their alternative name Pegasides (as perhaps also at Woodchester) or appear as haloed busts either end of the mosaic. Other Muses mosaics are suspected at Pit Meads and Bignor.

Neptune and Oceanus

Neptune/Poseidon was the god of freshwater and the sea. Oceanus was the god of the earth-circling ocean. In classical art Oceanus is identified by the lobster claws or crustacean legs emanating from his head. In Romano-British art the iconography of the two deities seems conflated and Neptune often appears thus crowned in myths where it can only be he who is portrayed. Thus at Pitney Neptune crowned with lobster claws approaches Amymone, who surrenders to him. On other mosaics from Hemsworth and Fordington, Dorset, or those at Verulamium and Rudston, one is never really certain who is being portrayed. It seems likely that in Britannia at least, just as Pan and Faunus became conflated so did Neptune and Oceanus. Thus Frampton's Neptune inscription with its 'Oceanus' mask refers to the same deity. Neptune from Ashcroft Villas, Cirencester, sports lobster claws and a trident in his hair. The mosaic included glass tesserae and may have paved an internal nymphaeum pool. He rode in his chariot in Cirencester's Dyer Street marine mosaic and overlooked Orpheus at Withington.

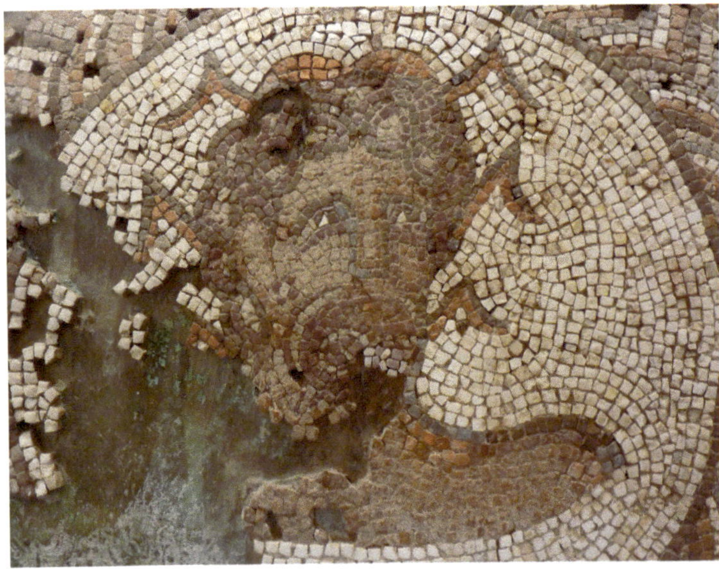

The Hemsworth Neptune bust in Dorchester Museum illustrates the likely quality of the missing Venus head. (Author's photograph)

Seasons

The Four Seasons appear on a number of Romano-British mosaics. Generally portrayed as busts, and female like their Greek predecessors, or as full-length *amorini* as at Chedworth, and mostly identified by their regular but changeable series of attributes. Occasionally they may have been represented by seasonal animals. They are usually arranged in a clockwise manner around the mosaic, often occupying the corners of the design. At Pitney *amorini* carrying *peda* (crooks) and attributes occupy panels in the centre of each side of a swastika-meander design. Unusually they are arranged as opposites with Winter facing Spring and Summer, Autumn. A similar opposite arrangement may exist at Lullingstone with Spring opposite to Autumn unless Autumn there wears corn rather than grapes. Sometimes identification is difficult when (as at Colliton Park, Dorchester) a complete set does not survive. Spring is commonly accompanied by a swallow/bird and either wears or carries flowers, leaves, a flower basket or chaplet. Summer has flowers, corn ears, poppies, leaves, flower basket, chaplet or a sickle. Autumn has grapes, possibly corn, a basket, pruning knife, shears or rake. Winter is generally portrayed wearing the hooded woollen cloak known as the *birrus Britannicus*. She holds a bare branch, or lime stick with a limed bird hanging from it, a cruel practice that provided a winter source of food. At Chedworth the cloaked *amorino* holds a dead hare and a branch. A very odd mosaic from Toft Green, York, that has undergone restoration perhaps both in Roman and modern times has three mediocre busts and a beautifully depicted Winter holding a branch. Bizarrely this figure is naked apart from a *chlamys* (cloak) on its shoulder, which raises questions as to its ancient identification. At Littlecote, seasonal divinities and animals encircle Orpheus.

Seasons with Bellerophon groups represent the turning of a year. The same interpretation may be given to the mosaic at Rudston where a central panel of a victorious charioteer refers to the iconography of Sol Invictus ('Unconquered Sun') around whom the seasons turn. At Itchen Abbas, Hampshire, and Whittlebury, Northamptonshire, single female busts may portray seasons but probably depict Flora, goddess of flowers, and winged Victoria. The tip of a palm branch remained at the top right-hand corner of the latter's panel.

Venus

Venus, goddess of beauty, spring and regeneration, was a popular subject for mosaics. Her emblems were the dove, scallop, rose, lotus, myrtle, fan and peacock feather (symbol of incorruptibility). Her lotus symbolised regeneration, dying into the mud each winter and emerging in spring. Like her, it was emblematic of spring and its leaf, used as a fan, was held by her or accompanied her image as at Frampton and Hemsworth. It suited the waterborne goddess, of 'good sailing', and lotus flowers and buds often accompany Venus on mosaics. Popular depictions showed her triumph or birth voyage to Cyprus on a shell, washing, putting on a sandal, and drying her hair (*Venus Anadyomene*). In art, both the scallop and the dove represent her while her son, Cupid, and dolphins act as supporters. Her marine *thiasus* includes *amorini*, tritons and nereids.

Hemsworth's unique apsidal mosaic depicts Venus standing within a shell blown to shore by lotus-leaf fans. She clasps her billowing garment while shielding her groin in a traditional

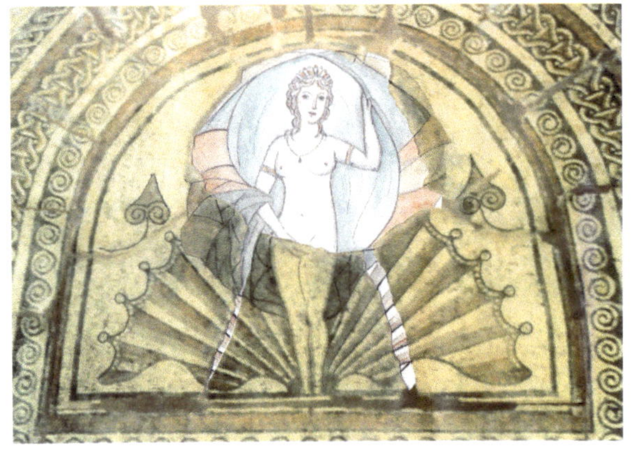

The Hemsworth Venus restored by the author after the Sabratha relief on a colourised photograph of 1908. Since painting, cleaning of the mosaic at the British Museum has shown that some garment folds differ from this interpretation. (Author's collection)

'display mode' as seen (in mirror image) and, minus the shell, on a bas relief of the Judgement of Paris on the proscenium wall at Sabratha, Libya. Botticelli's *Birth of Venus* has made the image of Venus standing in a shell so commonplace that it is a surprise to realise that the Hemsworth image appears to be unique among Roman mosaics. The author's previous iconographical research into Venus only located reclining or seated shell-borne goddesses, apart from a small terracotta in Agrigento Museum (Inv. 522). Hemsworth's goddess' feet are cut off at the ankles and perhaps evidence of the figure's prefabrication. Her legs show foreshortening as if to give the approaching viewer the *trompe l'oeil* effect that she was standing. The surrounding dolphins are also designed to appear upright and three dimensional.

A kneeling shell-borne Venus features on Horkstow's Medallions Mosaic. Rudston's wild, highly coloured and bizarre marine Venus is accompanied by a triton holding a torch (the symbol of life), suitable for the goddess of regeneration. Presumably abstracted from a shell group, she is portrayed as seated but without a shell to sit on. Her hair blows out in the *anadyomene* style and she clasps her golden apple. Venus' hand mirror appears by her side, often carried by Cupid in marine scenes. Her pubic area is boldly indicated by a red and white V-shape.

A leaf/fan and diadem identifies Venus at Frampton. Presumably here she boasted the cleft chin that was a trademark of that mosaicist. The Neptune and Cupid mosaic from the same villa featured corner panels featuring Venus including the Judgement of Paris, the Death of Adonis and the Admonition of Cupid. She appears in a symbolic pool with lotus leaves and holding her mirror at Kingscote. On Low Ham's Dido and Æneas mosaic she appears in all her regalia and with *amorini* holding torches of life and death. Mercury joins her at Pitney. The figures on this sadly lost mosaic were 5 feet in height and possibly prefabricated. They may have been wrongly placed in the design as Venus is in display mode and Paris, shown with hand to his chin (his traditional thinking pose for awarding the golden apple), might be expected to be viewing her. He, however, is placed with a nymph, who may be his first love Oenone. Venus had an affair with Mercury (seen here with caduceus and purse) with whom she had Hermaphroditus. However, he also loved the nymph Larunda and so might well instead be paired with Paris' companion! A bust from Thenford may represent Venus as a personification of spring as may a full-breasted figure with a necklace on Bratton Seymour's recently discovered mosaic.

15

Bellerophon Mosaics

Bellerophon and his half-brother the winged horse Pegasus' triumph over fire-breathing Chimaera occurs in Homer's *Iliad* (Book VI, 155–202), and was particularly popular in fourth-century Britannia, as five mosaics featuring it have been discovered here. These are from Boxford (Berkshire), Lullingstone (Kent), Croughton (Northamptonshire), Hinton St Mary and Frampton (Dorset). Considering that under thirty mosaics of the subject have been found throughout the empire the fact that five are British is interesting. The subject also appears in the late imperial palaces of Ravenna and Constantinople.

Bellerophon, Prince of Corinth and son of Poseidon/Neptune, was sent to Proetus, King of Tiryns, to be expiated for murder. Unfortunately Queen Anteia became besotted with him and, when rejected, told her husband that he had attempted to assault her. Forbidden by the laws of hospitality to kill his guest, Proetus sent him to Anteia's father, King Iobates, in Lycia with a letter requesting Bellerophon be put to death. The hospitable king left it too late to open the letter before the same laws of hospitality prevented him from killing

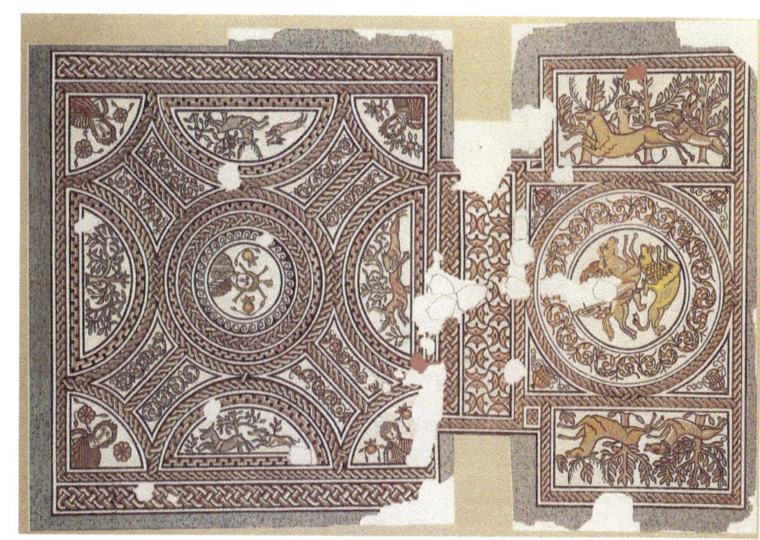

David Neal's recording of the Hinton St Mary mosaic with the Bellerophon roundel. (Copyright and courtesy of David S. Neal)

his guest. He therefore sent him to certain death, requesting that he rid the land of the monstrous Chimaera. She possessed a lion's body from which sprouted a goat's head and her tail was a living serpent. All heads breathed fire.

While in Corinth with Athena/Minerva's aid, Bellerophon tamed his half-brother Pegasus. Poseidon had seduced the beautiful Medusa in Athena's temple and so incensed the virgin goddess that she turned Medusa into the petrifying monster whose glance turned all to stone. When Perseus on his own quest beheaded the pregnant Medusa, her progeny, Pegasus and the humanoid Chrysaor, leapt fully grown from her neck. Pegasus (born at the *Pegae*, 'springs of the ocean') was a water symbol and could strike inspiring springs with his hoofs. On a Palmyran mosaic discovered in 2009 water uniquely streams from Pegasus' hoofs to drench Chimaera's flames. All British Bellerophons are either near rivers or on well-watered land. Bellerophon, riding Pegasus, destroyed Chimaera by thrusting a lead coated spear into the goat's mouth. The lead melted and killed her. After more trials Iobates relented and gave Bellerophon the hand of his daughter Philonoe.

Some Bellerophon mosaics such as Lullingstone's feature images of the Seasons. An ancient belief saw Pegasus as the sun and Chimaera as winter. Bellerophon, as the active power of the sun, attacks winter and thus arranges the sequence of the seasons. Bellerophon killing Chimaera also represented the power of good conquering evil and, as such, the image was adopted into early Christian art, gradually developing into St George and the Dragon. It thus seems particularly pertinent that the myth was popular in Britain. The image could be interpreted differently by pagans and Christians. In late antiquity a landowner might wish to be flatteringly identified with Bellerophon before his tenants and clients. It is notable that Bellerophon's pose (without Chimaera) is adopted by the Emperor Anastasius I on the Barberini Diptych in the Louvre. Pegasus was later catasterised by Zeus/Jupiter and at Croughton a row of stars above the group commemorates this honour. Bellerophon almost becomes a sky god with his connection with the sun and seasons and his transition to Christianity is displayed on an early fifth-century cut glass bowl made either in Constantinople or Rome and found in Jesuitengasse, Augsburg (Römisches Museum (Inv. 1983, 2325). It shows triumphant, weaponless Bellerophon (complete with nimbus and adopting the orans pose of a Christian worshipper) on Pegasus flying above the dead Chimaera, while a spring nymph pours water in front of the steed. Some German scholars have controversially seen Bellerophon here as representing Christ himself.

Bellerophon's combat appears on archaic Greek pottery from the seventh century BC and on early pebble mosaics from the fourth century BC. The basic composition hardly changed over the centuries with the heroically naked hero only wearing a *petasos* (hat), *cothurni* (boots) and a *chlamys* (cloak). However, by the later fourth century AD, he wears contemporary dress as at Boxford and Croughton with tunics fashionably decorated with *orbiculi* (roundels) at shoulder and thigh and (at Boxford) with *clavi* (stripes) at the neck.

The Hinton St Mary and Frampton Bellerophons are the work of the Durnovarian firm and earlier than those at Boxford and Croughton. As at Boxford, Hinton's Bellerophon group faced the entrance to the chamber. The workmanship is fine but lacking in vigour. Pegasus rather resembles a stringless marionette and is wingless while Chimaera is depicted in emotionless flight. She has an attractive imbricated mane in red and yellow and a speckled serpent tail. Both feature the heavy-lidded eyes often found in late Roman art, affording them a sedated look. Bellerophon is damaged but adopts the traditional pose and his *chlamys* billows out to the right. Both Pegasus and Chimaera feature the distinctive concertina-like muscles on the upper forelimb that are a trait of this mosaicist.

The inner section of Hinton's bipartite room has a central roundel facing in the opposite direction to Bellerophon featuring a male bust backed by the chi-rho symbol. Often identified as Christ, others see him as Constantine I or Magnentius backed by the *labarum*, the sacred military standard of the Christian emperors. Pomegranates, symbols of rebirth and fertility, flank his head. Four corner busts are identified as the Evangelists. All feature the dimpled chin and folded neck that identifies that mosaicist's work. A lunette featuring a tree, possibly the Tree of Life/Knowledge, marks the room's place of honour. A masonry bench is believed to have been set against the wall behind it. Hunting dogs and their prey in the mosaic's lunettes feature the concertina-muscled limbs. Discovered in 1963, the entire pavement was for decades displayed at the British Museum but, presumably to save space, only the head of 'Christ' is now exhibited.

Frampton's Bellerophon was the first discovered during the Lysons' excavations of 1796–97. Lysons believed the damaged group depicted a mounted lion hunt, but the discovery of the Hinton St Mary mosaic showed that it was another Durnovarian Bellerophon. Lysons misinterpreted the concertina muscles and spear into a spiral. Bellerophon here centred a mosaic bounded by a dolphin frieze with inscriptions to Neptune (his and Pegasus' father) and Cupid. Remaining corner panels featured scenes concerned with Venus: Paris and Venus, Venus and Adonis (a down-turned torch proclaims his death) and Cupid admonished by Venus. The outer part of the chamber featured a badly damaged depiction of Bacchus on a leopard's back, flanked by panels of hunting scenes. An apse faced the Neptune inscription floored with a mosaic depicting a symbolic pool and *cantharus* fountain. It included a chi-rho monogram in its threshold that was probably more an apotropaic symbol rather than a statement of Christianity.

Lullingstone's Bellerophon also features a connection to Neptune's realm. His combat takes place over a sea peopled with bulbous dolphins and flapping scallops, which is mythologically incorrect but may also refer to Pegasus' birth at the *pegae*. The villa's basement had also featured a water shrine. The dolphins are the type represented at Hemsworth and Fifehead Neville, but here are flat areas of colour and not designed to appear three dimensional. Pegasus and Bellerophon are elegantly if weakly drawn but the steed does sport the most believable wings of any British mount and has genitalia. Bellerophon in a red *chlamys* and *cothurni* elegantly spears the fleeing otter-like Chimaera below them. Their cushion-like panel is cornered by the Seasons, the only British Bellerophon mosaic to show them. Beyond a textile-like patterned mosaic carpet (perhaps aping an actual covering) the great tessellated raised apse of this room designed for a large *stibadium* dining couch overlooked a beautiful panel depicting the Rape of Europa. The abducted heroine sits elegantly on the joyously bouncing bull that is Jupiter above a wine-dark sea while Pothos (sexual desire) with his torch leads the way to Crete. Another *amorino* hangs onto the bull's tail perhaps to restrain him or to enjoy the ride. Its inscription translates as 'If jealous Juno had seen the swimmings of the bull, more justly would she have gone to the halls of Æolus' and refers to a passage in Virgil's Æneid when Juno asks the wind god Æolus to send a storm to destroy Æneas' fleet. The inscription has spawned several theories seeing it as a Christian cryptogram that includes the names of the villa owner, Avitas, and Jesus. Interestingly its first Latin word 'Invida' (jealous) was employed as a charm against the evil eye at the

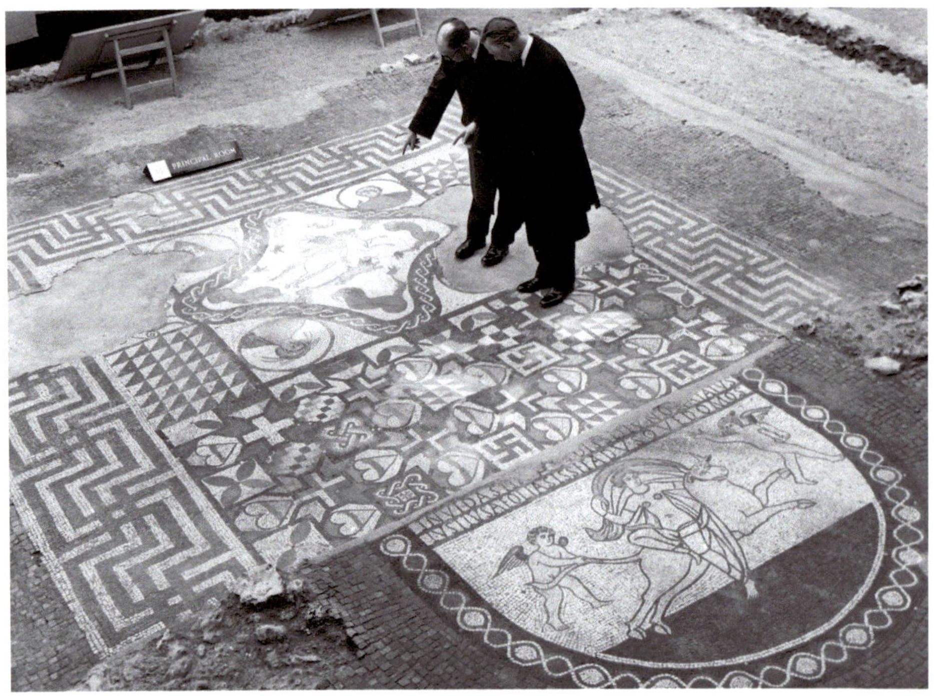

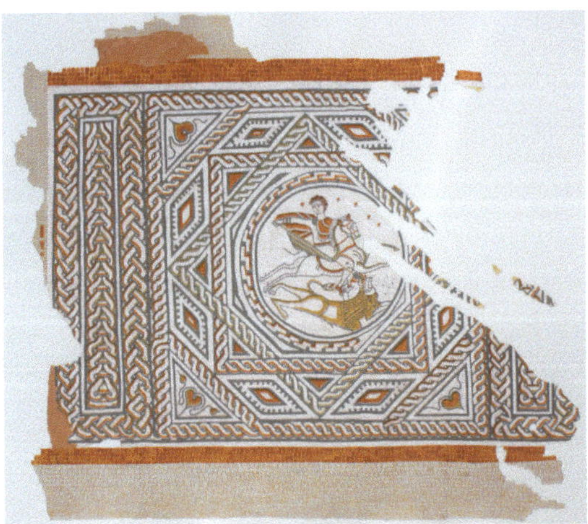

Above: Lullingstone villa's excavator Lieutenant-Colonel G. W. Meates explaining the Bellerophon mosaic to Richard Sharples, of the Ministry of Works, on the opening of the new cover building, 2 April 1963. (Author's collection)

Left: David Neal's recording of the Croughton Bellerophon. Note the mosaicists' bad centring of the roundel. (Courtesy and copyright David S. Neal)

beginning of fourth-century North African inscriptions. Lullingstone with its house church and *stibadium* is Britain's strongest contender for a Christian Bellerophon mosaic.

Croughton's Bellerophon wears contemporary fourth- to fifth-century dress with a belted white tunic with *orbiculi* (roundels) and a red *chlamys*. Notwithstanding the depiction's naivety, it was, until the discovery of the Boxford mosaic, the most spirited of the British Bellerophon panels. Bellerophon looks away, spearing Chimaera in her lion mouth as she turns to attack. Her mane is heavy and composed of ochre tesserae. The goat head and serpent tail are poorly delineated but attack the hero. Pegasus is depicted in linear style with flipper-like wings and a mane distantly reminiscent of Boxford's. This circular panel is badly centred within interlaced squares, which might suggest that the panel was prefabricated and wrongly placed or that a serious mistake was made in laying out the design before starting.

The most beautiful, spirited and painterly British Bellerophon panel is that excavated at Boxford in 2017–19. It faced the southern entrance to the room and was the first image viewed by visitors. Bellerophon, in a white tunic, has lost both his head and leg. His *chlamys* billows out in front and his shoulder is outlined in white. He plunges his spear towards Chimaera's goat head. Pegasus is laid in ochre tesserae with blue outline and muscles. His magnificent mane and tail are composed of contrasting rows of long thin tesserae in ochre and blue. In line with the other *trompe l'oeil* effects on this mosaic he is foreshortened to achieve perspective and his front legs overlap the guilloche border showing the underside of the hoofs. His hind legs taper, cutting across and terminating an inscription in a neighbouring panel, giving the impression that he is flying out of the mosaic at an angle. He has long striped wings with extending flight feathers and red harness fittings and straps. Above is a panel inscribed 'BELLEREFONS', a spelling remarkably only known from one mosaic found at the Villa de Puerta Oscura, Malaga, Spain. Pegasus' name box sits beneath him. Albeit damaged, Chimaera is a splendid creation, almost heraldic, and based on the Cithaeronian lion in the mosaic's west border. Turning to attack, she shoots fire from all three heads, although only part of the serpent's jaw and throat survives. Uniquely she is provided with a row of teats along her belly. Her name box may have fitted below Pegasus' front legs. At Boxford the connection noted elsewhere with Poseidon/Neptune is very strong and also connects with the mosaic's other myths such as Arion, Pelops and (through Chrysaor's son Geryon) to Hercules.

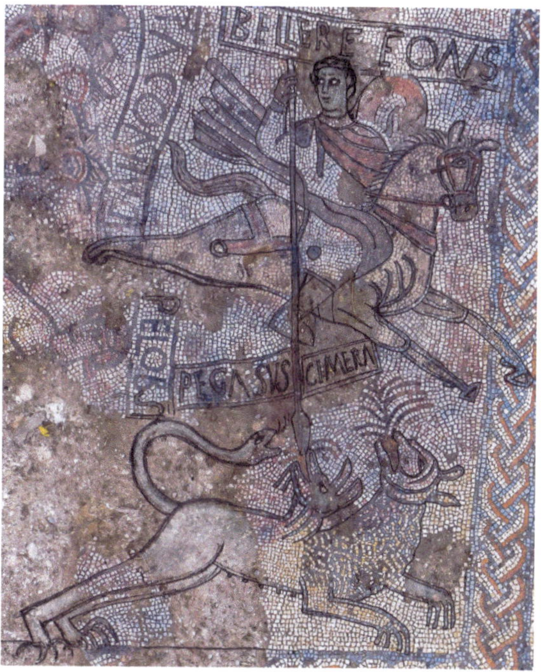

Author's interpretative reconstruction of the Boxford Bellerophon. (Author's collection)

16

Orpheus Mosaics

Mosaics depicting the musician Orpheus, son of the Muse Calliope and the Thracian king Oeagrus, were particularly popular in Britannia, where a disproportionally high number have been discovered compared to other provinces. A type developed here that is all but unique in the Roman world showing Orpheus surrounded by concentric circles of animals. The inspiration for this is likely to have been the internal decoration of bowls or painted vault decoration such as at the Thracian tomb at Kazanlak, Bulgaria. Orpheus' story was attractive. Raised among the Muses on Mount Parnassus, the god Apollo, whom he adored, gave him a lyre and taught him to play. His music and singing could charm all creatures and even coax trees and rocks into dance. Rivers could change course as they danced. He visited and returned from the underworld in his quest to restore his beloved wife Eurydice and there his music had power over Hades/Pluto. He joined and aided the Argonauts in the quest for the Golden Fleece. After losing Eurydice he gave up the love of women and turned to boys to enjoy their youth but eventually was torn to pieces by Maenads (Bacchantes) for rejecting them and not sufficiently honouring Dionysos/Bacchus. Orpheus' lyre or *kithara* was catasterised by Zeus and became the constellation Lyra. The Orphic mystery cult is believed to have regarded Orpheus as a parallel figure to or even an incarnation of Bacchus/ Dionysos. Dionysos Zagreus (son of Zeus and Persephone) suffered an identical death, being torn to pieces by the Titans and then reassembled and reborn as the son of Zeus and Semele. Orpheus like Bellerophon was adopted into the iconography of Christianity as representing David or the Good Shepherd and his image appears in Christian catacombs. In AD 508 the synagogue at Gaza was decorated with a depiction labelled 'David' adapted from an Orpheus design complete with wild animals.

Like Christ, Orpheus descended and returned from the underworld to save his beloved, in the former's case the 'faithful'. Orpheus thus became a symbol of victory over death, and symbolic of eternal life. Thracians believed in immortality and death was but an episode. Like Bellerophon it is possible that villa owners might wish others to see themselves and their might personified in Orpheus. Wearing Eastern costume and the Phrygian cap, Orpheus plays a lyre or *kithara* and is generally accompanied by a fox, a creature that lives both above and below ground. The sagacious fox also links him with Bacchus, whose epithet Bassareus is a Thracian name for Dionysus, derived from *bassaris* (fox skin), worn by his devotees in the cult mysteries. Several Orphic mosaics such as those at Newton St Loe, Whatley or Panik (Bosnia Hercegovina) are adjacent to portrait panels depicting the goddess Ceres/Demeter, who often wears a *modius* (corn measure) on her head. Ceres, goddess of agriculture, was also a chthonic deity. These busts' identities are disputed but Ceres/Demeter was widely worshiped as an earth goddess who promised rebirth. Sparta knew her as Demeter-Chthonia (chthonic Demeter). She presided over the Eleusinian mystery cult promising initiates a blessed afterlife much as did the Orphic and Bacchic cults and later the Christian. Hence her juxtapositioning to Orpheus is explained.

The majority of foreign Orpheus mosaics show Orpheus surrounded by subdued animals on a single field. The mosaic at Brading on the Isle of Wight is of this type where he commands the rapt attention of a monkey, two birds, a hare and a fox. Set in a coarse, chequered, porticus floor, it is the first mosaic that visitors to the house would have encountered. Orpheus sits within a guilloche-bordered roundel set within a square guilloche frame. J. P. Emslie's lithograph records fragmentary crude linear heads and tendrils at the corners. It is uncertain whether these faced inwards or outwards. If outwards, then facial lines make sense as eyebrows and nose and what would otherwise be the 'shoulders' of an inward-looking head may well be head wings and the subject the Four Winds. Otherwise the Seasons is a possibility. Their crudity reminds one of the Seasons mosaic at Bignor and one might suggest that this mosaic is also third century.

The Whatley mosaic was found in 1837 and is only recorded by a poor lithograph by Hill, a drawing and indistinct photographs. It appears to have been a variant of the continental mosaics with Orpheus occupying a square panel, presumably with his fox and perhaps a tree or birds. It occupied the pivoting point of an L-shaped apsidal chamber. Echoing the British circular mosaics, the presumed Orpheus square was surrounded by a border of

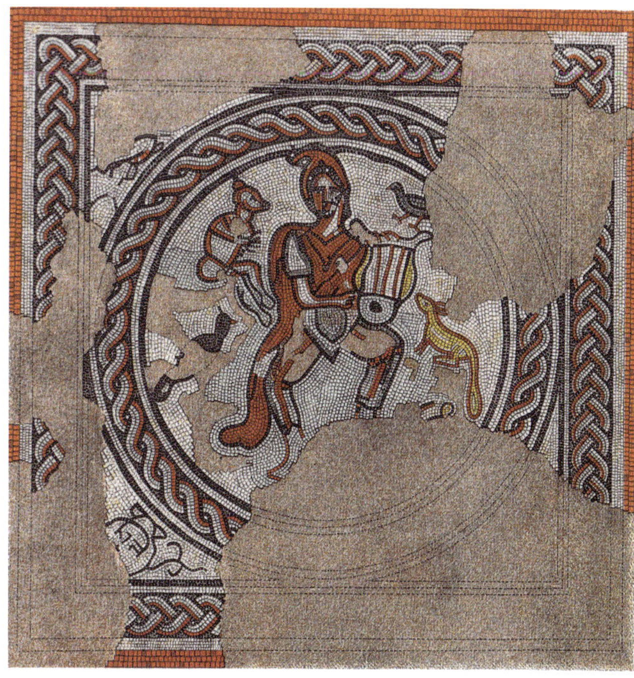

Brading villa's Orpheus panel
as recorded on excavation
by J. P. Emslie, 1881.
(Author's collection)

confronted animals, as at Newton St Loe, interspersed with trees and small bushes. Long ridiculed for the appearance of the elephant and other animals on the lithograph, the other sources suggest that Hill and not the mosaicist was to blame and that the menagerie was acceptably naturalistic. The apse featured a small lunette-shaped symbolic pool holding a fish/dolphin (photographed in 1928 and close to the lithograph in appearance). This was topped by four trapezoidal compartments (garden beds) containing planted *canthari*. Although a cover building was erected and still survived in 1906, visitors unpicked much of the mosaic before its collapse or demolition.

The other part of the chamber featured a bust in a roundel wearing either a *modius* or a mural crown with three unevenly spaced towers, which might suggest her to be either Ceres, Cybele or a Tyche. The central 'tower' appears taller. A visitor to the site in 1864 commented:

The pavement is of the usual small tesserae, with little red and black in ornament, with figures of elephant, lion etc, in places injured but on the whole tolerably perfect. A head of Ceres with cornucopia and fish is the best part. A drawing was shown to aid in understanding it which might be much better than it is.

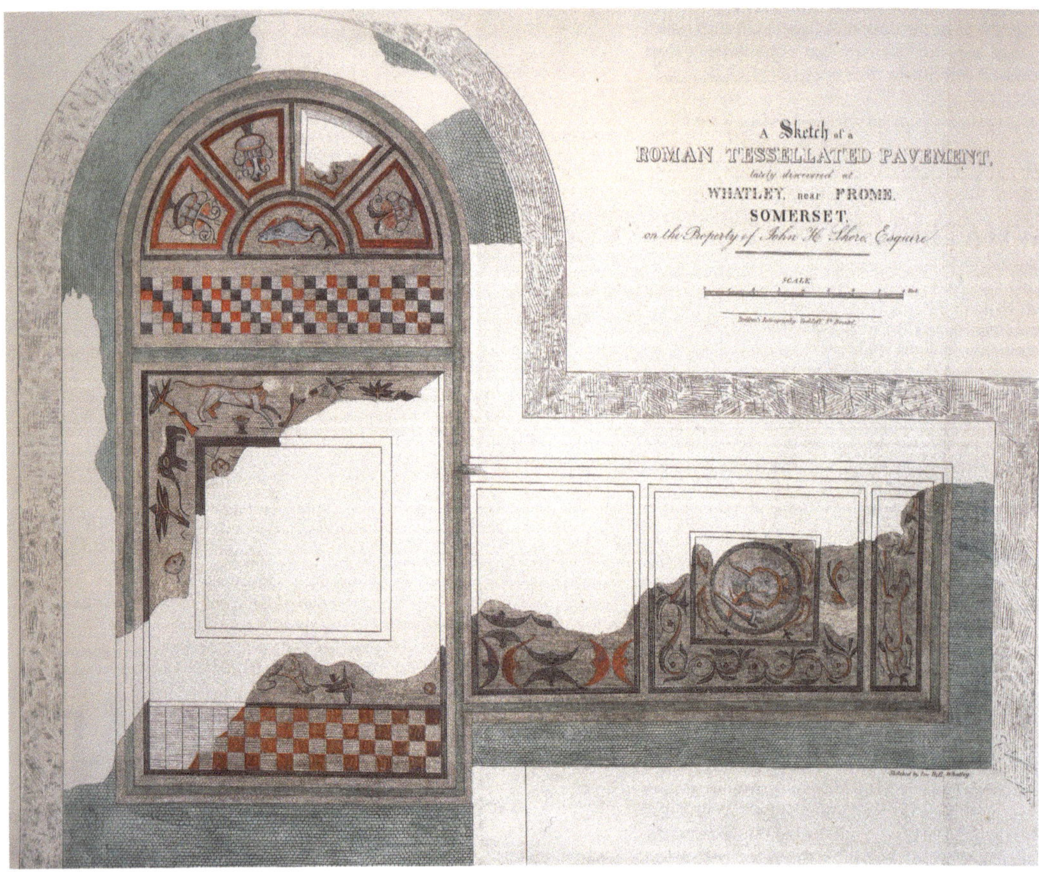

John Hill's engraving of Whatley villa's mosaic. (Author's collection)

76

Traces of a divine halo around the head are suggested on the lithograph and drawing copied for the *Victoria County History of Somerset* (Volume 1). Dolphins sport in the corners of her surrounding panel. Beyond the bust a marine panel featured fish and a *pardalocampus* confronting a *capricornus*.

The concentric circle Orpheus mosaics that were so popular with patrons and virtually unique to Britain are exemplified by the finest at Woodchester attributed to the Corinian workshop. Romano-British mosaicists seem to have developed the design to make it their own and several firms obviously catered for the demand. A mosaic from Salona (Croatia) dating from the late second to early third century gives us the first step to the later design. Here a common indented-square design has a central circular panel featuring Orpheus. A concentric circle, divided into six segments occupied by birds, surrounds Orpheus. A similar segmented radial circle surrounds Bacchus on the late third-century Thruxton mosaic. Four animals occupy boxes in the Salona spandrels and the lunettes hold sea beasts, thus covering air, land and water. There are no known Orphic concentric examples after this until the British fourth-century mosaics. An Orpheus mosaic from Merida (Spain) illustrates a rare European spin-off from the British design and may be a rough guide as to the appearance of Pit Meads' possible Orphic pavement. Birds and animals occupy its concentric circle.

The Woodchester Orpheus pavement is the largest known mosaic north of the Alps and one of the marvels of Roman Britain. Measuring 15 metres square, it floored a great columned reception room with a central fountain. It displays the highly skilled work of the Corinian firm and must, with their other mosaics there, have been a huge commission. It was previously uncovered every ten years and displayed to the public but has been buried since 1973. Unfortunately the manpower willingly available to uncover it evaporated when it was time to rebury it. Faced with such a huge quantity of earth to move, a mechanical digger had to be employed. The author has been informed by several archaeological colleagues that, disastrously, the hypocaust collapsed under its weight. It is not known what damage was inflicted on the mosaic.

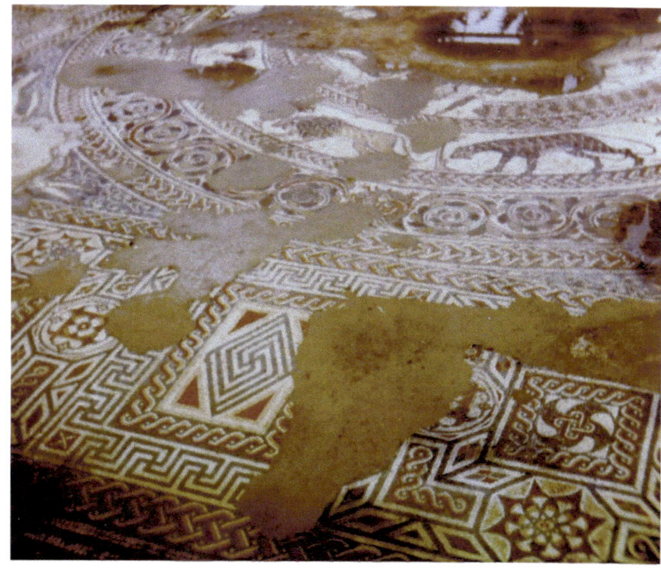

The Woodchester Orpheus mosaic as displayed in 1973. (Author's photograph)

First noted around 1693, the mosaic suffered at the hands of grave diggers for centuries. Some exposed portions were recorded by antiquarians before they were destroyed by frost, but by 1973 around 42 per cent of the mosaic remained. Beyond the four column bases occupying the spandrels of the central Orpheus pavement a frame of twenty-four square geometric mosaic panels (each sufficiently large enough to form the centrepiece of a room) form an ambulatory around the room. The centre of the floor featured an octagonal guilloche band with an off-centre figure of Orpheus occupying its southern side. Indirect evidence for the robbing of lead pipes and the strong onsite springs suggest a lost central fountain pool reputedly containing a mosaic decorated with sea denizens. The presence of eight water nymphs at the spandrels alludes to Orpheus' ability to charm waters or the Pegasides of Helicon. Orpheus, his fox, birds and bushes occupy the first circular zone that is bordered by a bay-laurel garland and a guilloche band. They are encircled by a second zone occupied by a music-sedated menagerie of fierce animals of the hunt and arena (including a gryphon) that plod in a clockwise procession around Orpheus. The lost elephant displayed a highly stylised 'netted' body pattern used in Roman art to indicate its wrinkled skin. The mosaicists' shading and treatment of the animals is very fine and they are interspersed with trees and faintly backed by pale bushes as if to impart depth to the scene. The Orphic charm thus captures denizens of water, air and land including trees and streams. The zone is encircled by a wonderful acanthus scroll, one of the firm's specialities. It issues from the mouth of a bearded horned figure often called Oceanus but more likely to be Achelous, god of all waters, who evolved into the medieval Green Man, and also had chthonic associations in ancient Greece. This chthonic aspect reflects those of the Orphic

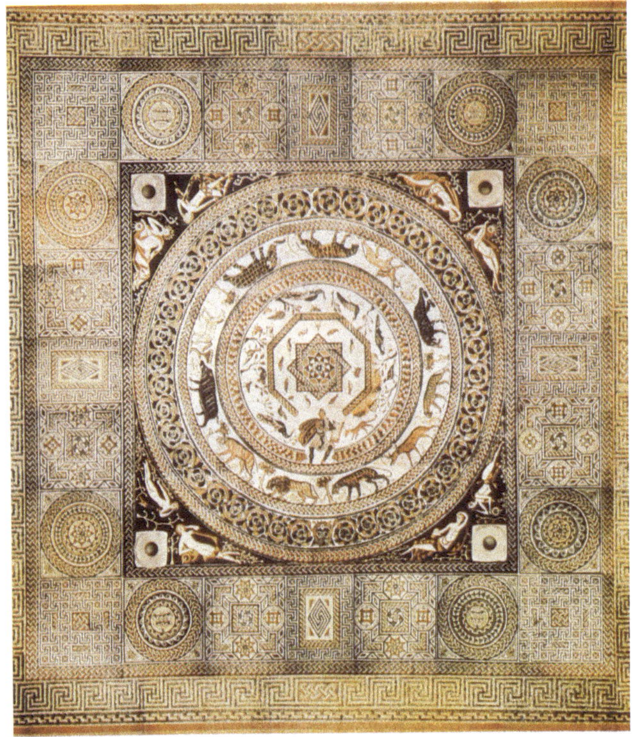

The wonderful recreation by the Woodward brothers of the Orpheus mosaic displays the magnificence of the original. (Author's collection)

mysteries. David Smith noted a copy of one of the surrounding geometric panels in the Imperial palace at Trier and believed the firm had gained a future commission there.

In the 1980s John and Bob Woodward researched and undertook the colossal task of creating a facsimile of the mosaic as it might have appeared when perfect. This stunning work of love permitted the world to appreciate how superb the room would have appeared in antiquity. At first the replica was displayed in a disused chapel in Wotton-under-Edge, but this proved too small and it was subsequently exhibited at various venues throughout the country. Lacking a permanent home, it was later sold and 'lost' to the public but has recently re-emerged and hopefully will one day be displayed again.

In 1824, Barton Farm, Cirencester, produced another smaller concentric circles Orpheus mosaic by the same mosaicists. Here Orpheus and his fox occupied the central roundel encircled by a clockwise procession of birds. At Woodchester the birds do not process but face in both directions. Beyond an encircling bay-laurel wreath wild beasts pace. These are so similar to those at Woodchester that the mosaicists must have worked from a standard cartoon/pattern. A lost Orpheus mosaic, probably by the same firm or in their style, is now only known from a drawing. It was found in 1820 at No. 93 Dyer Street, Cirencester (a cheesemonger's), and a rough sketch was made of it at the time from which an engraving was produced in 1886. We do not know its condition at the time of discovery and the drawing may have been tidied up and the square of its borders completed for the engraving. The mosaic's authenticity has been questioned by some and it is claimed to be a garbled copy of that from Barton Farm, but this ignores several intriguing aspects of it. Beecham had no doubts of its authenticity. The central roundel holds Orpheus and his fox in an off-centre position suggesting that, as at Woodchester, they strayed into the encircling bird zone, which is again bound by a laurel wreath. Beyond this a concentric circle holds beasts plodding clockwise. This circle is bounded by an unusual meander border that was also found on a mosaic from Parsonage Field, Cirencester, in 1958 but does not appear elsewhere

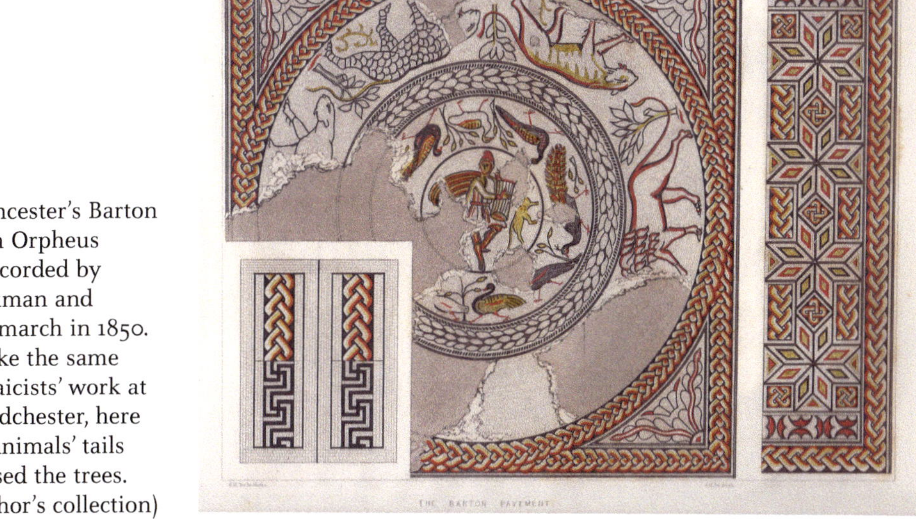

Cirencester's Barton Farm Orpheus as recorded by Buckman and Newmarch in 1850. Unlike the same mosaicists' work at Woodchester, here the animals' tails crossed the trees. (Author's collection)

in the town. Beecham reports this to have been worked in 'green, buff, red and black'. The outer border apparently had guilloche and panels of meander and the spandrels had rosettes and laurel sprays. What is particularly interesting is a central figure above Orpheus that is a representation of the sea monster Scylla ('Violence'). She holds a weapon and a steering oar and has three tails as depicted in the Baths of Neptune, Ostia (or the central one was a misinterpretation by the sketcher of her fringed dog apron). A panther-like animal also in the central panel may have actually been a *pardalocampus* and, like Woodchester's, the roundel may have represented water. Scylla is unknown on British mosaics and her image is rare and unlikely to have been known to a Cirencester cheesemonger or townsman in 1820, which makes her presence here indirect proof of the mosaic's authenticity. Her inclusion, although unknown in foreign Orphic mosaics, shows that Orpheus calms even the violence of Scylla. It cannot be proven that Scylla did not also feature in the lost central marine panel at Woodchester. She may be a British inclusion in the repertory symbolising brutish violence as does the centaur on some foreign Orpheus mosaics.

Littlecote's unique Orpheus mosaic was discovered in 1727, reburied in 1730, and rediscovered in 1977 by Bryn Walters and Bernard Philips, who later excavated it. It had suffered greatly since reburial but was fully restored in 1979–80 using the 1730 engraving by George Vertue as the guide. It floored a bipartite ceremonial building with a triconchial western end, dated by the excavators to AD 360–362 and claimed to be the earliest example of what would become a standard pattern for Byzantine churches. The building, adjacent to a bath suite, seems to have been used as a private space for a syncretic cult of Orpheus, Apollo and Dionysos/Bacchus. Orpheus had suffered the same death as the young Dionysos-Zagreus in being torn to pieces. The latter transformed himself into a series of animal disguises when fleeing from the Titans and four of these circle the figure

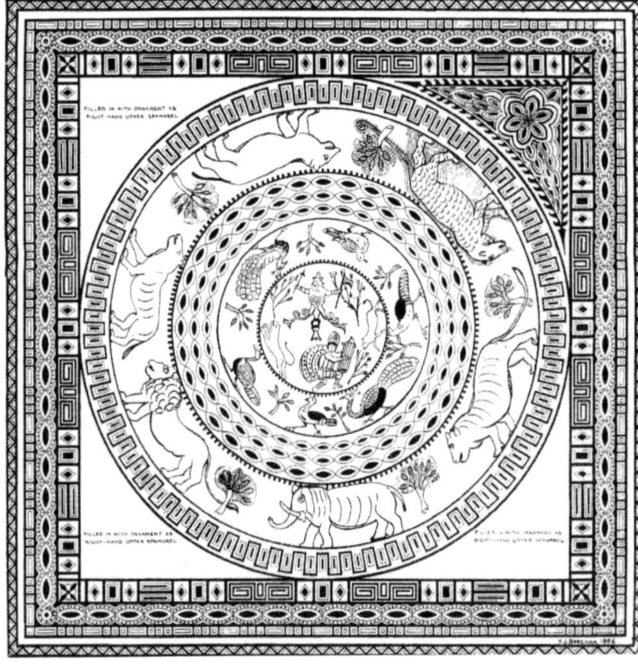

The 1820 Dyer Street Orpheus with the central figure of Scylla. as engraved by K. J. Beecham. (Author's collection)

of Orpheus and his fox in the central roundel. Here at Littlecote Orpheus conflates and assumes the mantle of Apollo and Dionysos/Bacchus.

Four seasonal goddesses dance around the circle in the manner of the Horae (the deities who cause the seasons to change). Aphrodite/Venus, goddess of spring and renewal, gazes in her mirror accompanied by a hind, while Nemesis, goddess of retribution, holding her goose accompanies a panther and represents summer. Nemesis is sometimes credited as Helen of Troy's mother rather than Leda, with whom this figure has also been identified, holding the swan that was Zeus. Demeter/Ceres, goddess of agriculture representing autumn and motherhood, accompanies a bull. Her most common attributes are wheat stalks, a flaming torch, poppies, the caduceus of Pax (Peace) or millet stalks, symbols of prosperity and fertility. Here, however, the restoration follows Vertue and she holds a vine stock which, if accurately recorded, perhaps alludes to her cult companion Dionysos and that, when the bull (Zagreus) was torn to pieces by the Titans, she saved its heart. Demeter gave it to Zeus and Zagreus was reborn as Dionysos from his union with Semele. Demeter's daughter, Persephone, Queen of the Underworld, represents winter and death. She waves goodbye to her mother to spend her season in Hades and is accompanied by the goat representing her son Zagreus.

The three scallop-like apsidal mosaics actually depict the underside of panther skins such as appear on a Bacchic wine cup in the Hildesheim treasure. The rays may indeed be intended to represent the setting sun, but the chequered pelts appear at the wavy edges. Panther heads stare out at worshippers who would have been seated on curving benches set on the coarse borders, the apses being too small to accommodate dining couches. The effect must have resembled the disciples sat on a curved bench on the twelfth-century Pentecostal mosaic at Monreale cathedral, Sicily.

A panel depicting a *cantharus* flanked by Dionysian/Bacchic *pardalocampi* spans the eastern end of the chamber. These and the attendant dolphins may refer to the episode of the Tyrrhenian pirates and the god's vengeance. Beyond a fine four-panelled lotus-flower mosaic a second *cantharus* is flanked by a pair of female panthers and backed by vines. The panther was

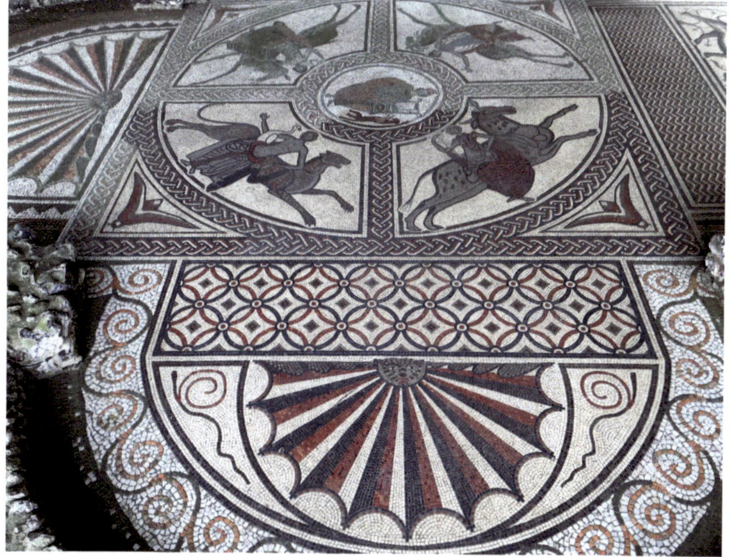

Littlecote, Wiltshire. The 'chancel' of the Orphic building from a side apse showing the seasonal goddesses, the speckled panther skins and the symbolic pool to the right. (Courtesy of Luigi Thompson)

Dionysos' companion and drank from his wine cup. They stand by a symbolic pool indicated by its zig-zag water pattern commonly found throughout the empire but rarely in Britain.

The badly damaged Orpheus mosaic at Horkstow is one of three panels that once filled a great hall measuring around 18 m x 8 m. All were elaborate and their designer exceeded the technical expertise of the mosaicists engaged to bring them to fruition. They are, notwithstanding, of great importance. The Orpheus panel appears to be a stylised development from the large third-century circular mosaic at Volubilis, Morocco. There eight large trees circle a 'park' and radiate towards its central polygonal panel holding Orpheus. The trunks divide it into segments and spreading branches create arcs within which animals and birds are placed and wander in different directions. At Horkstow, radiating arms of guilloche replace the trees, thus forming the spokes of a wheel-like design.

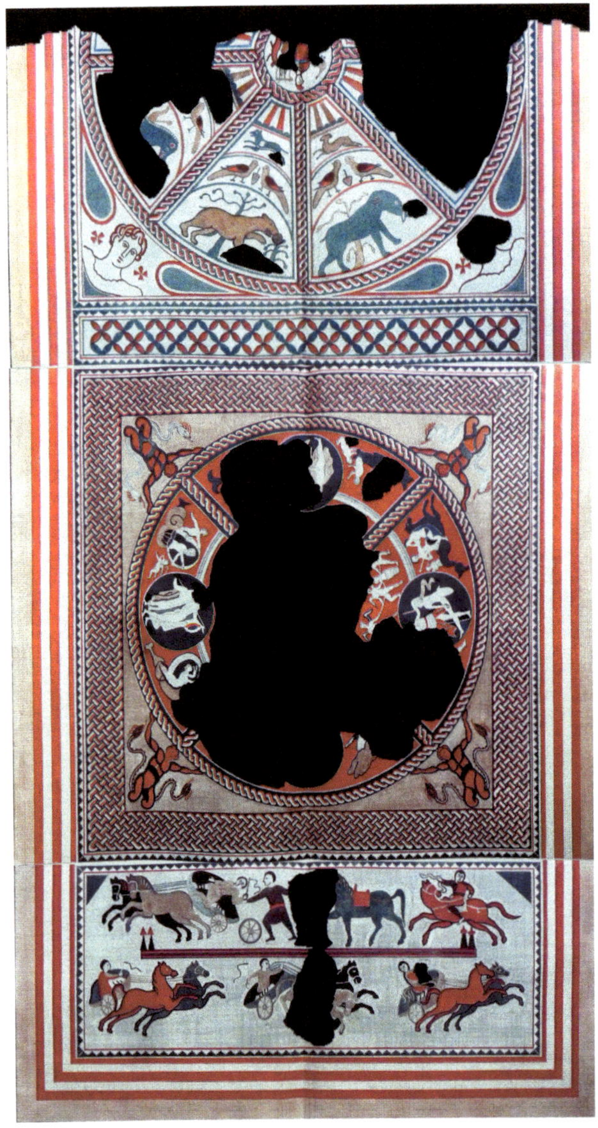

A montage of Lysons' separate recordings of the Horkstow mosaic illustrates its original design and complexity. (Author's collection)

Orpheus and his fox occupy the hub that is fringed with a contrastingly coloured scallop design. The fox turns his back on Orpheus here and a peacock, symbol of rejuvenation, accompanies them. Orpheus possibly faced the doorway to the chamber to the south. Simple arcs join the wheel spokes, creating in each trapezoidal compartment three zones. The outer ones are occupied by large quadrupeds, a boar, bear and elephant, who move anticlockwise around while the central arcs have confronted birds either side of bunches of grapes. Finally animals of the hunt, a hound and a hare (or doe) run clockwise around the circle. The large animals are backed by trees referring not only to a landscape but also echoing the tradition of placing sculpture in front of trees in Roman gardens. Similarly placed trees appear elsewhere on mosaics such as the running hunting dog at Cherhill, Wiltshire. Unidentified busts, probably seasons, occupy the spandrels outside Horkstow's circle. Hooded winter does not survive to elucidate their sequence.

Adjacent to the Orpheus panel was the Medallions Mosaic that the author has identified as an Achilles cycle, depicting major episodes from his life within four medallions. These were set on a zoned design of concentric circles divided into four sections by guilloche spokes, each holding a medallion. Like Achilles' life it was one of contrasts – love and loss, life and death – and may be loosely based on his shield as described in the *Iliad*. That was full of contrasts, showing peace and war, work and festival in different zones and centred by the sun and the heavens. The mosaic's shield is held aloft by four anguipede (snake-legged) giants. Unusually the backgrounds are coloured red and ochre and the 'jewelled' medallions black. The dipping of Achilles in the Styx by his mother was possibly countered by another medallion showing his death whereas another depicting his love for Deidameia (or Patroclus) was countered by his killing of his last love Penthesilea. The zones either side of the medallions echoed their emotions. Thus the medallion of the romance was bordered on one side by Venus in her scallop shell whereas adjacent to the Penthesilea medallion a triton comforts a weeping nereid in a traditional mourning pose while an *amorino* jockey holds on to the reins of her *hippocampus*. In the medallion the usually naked hero is clothed in a tunic and belted corslet as is a similarly armoured Achilles on the recently found *intaglio* of the same scene from Tossal de Baltarga, Spain. Penthesilea is depicted sprawled with her aggressor holding her by the hair. She seemingly holds a sword but adopts the 'fatal pose' only used in art by those about to be dispatched. A rod once crossed her leg, perhaps the handle of her *labrys* or double axe. In a zone above the nereid group, dancing *amorini* bind a *baetylus* (sacred stone) or grave marker with ribbons. A flower basket stands before it. Possibly the central circle held an image of Sol/ Apollo the sun in deference to Homer's shield. Interestingly the mosaic's spoked and zonal arrangement bears a simplified resemblance to those postulated by Alexander Pope and John Flaxman in their attempts to illustrate Homer's description of the shield.

Beyond the Medallions Mosaic a chariot race may refer to the funerary games given for Achilles or Patroclus and to 'The Racecourse of Achilles', an ancient name for his isle of immortality, Leuke, in the Black Sea. Contemporary cults saw both Orpheus and Achilles connected with rebirth, hence their juxtapositioning here. After his 'death' by Paris' arrow, Thetis gave Achilles an island created by Poseidon on which to live. The island was Leuke (White Island) to the Greeks, and Alba to the Romans. According to Lucius Flavius Arrianus (Arrian), it was also called 'The Island of Achilles'. Because of his connection with rebirth Achilles cycles also ornamented sarcophagi. White Island

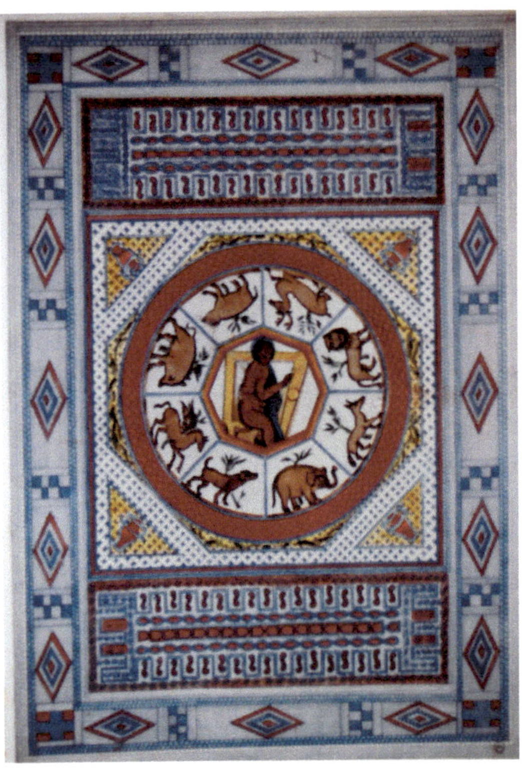

Left: The Winterton Orpheus as recorded in the 1790s. (Author's collection)

Below: The many hundreds of pieces of the Newton St Loe Orpheus panel in Bristol Museum put together by the author in 2000. (Author's photograph)

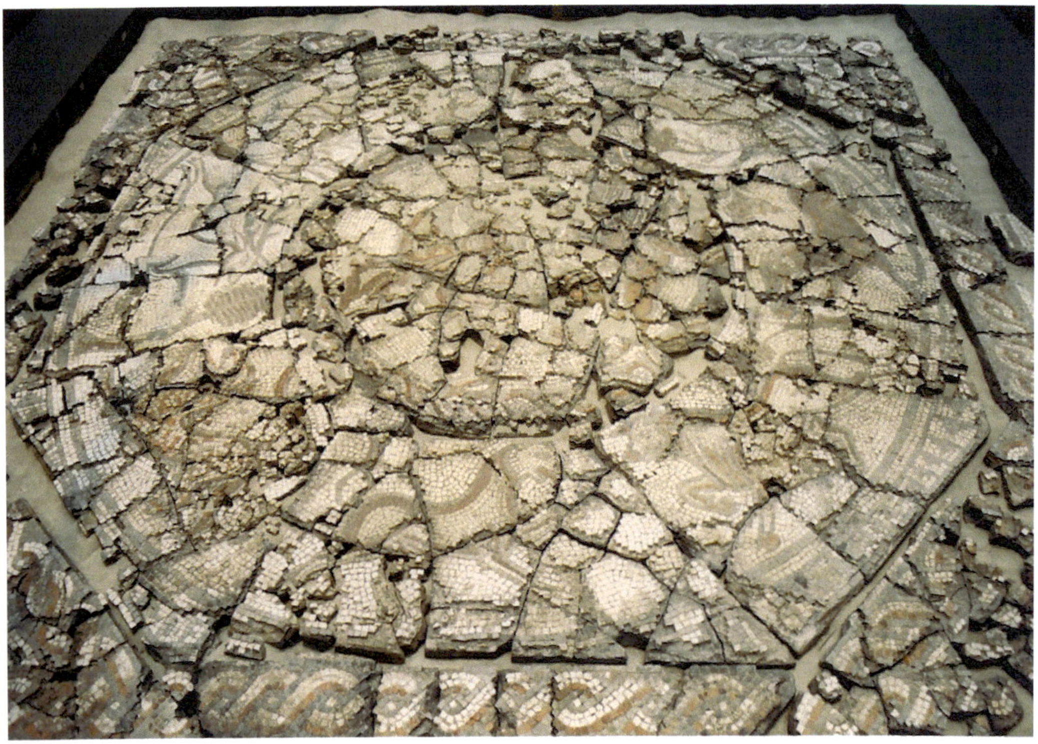

held a temple to Achilles and Patroclus and also shrines to the Thracian Apollo, beloved of Orpheus.

The concentric Orpheus mosaic from nearby Winterton was set within an octagon and a guilloche square. *Canthari* filled the spandrels and the panel was framed either end by rectangular geometric panels. Excavated in 1747, it was poorly recorded and then fell prey to country people. About a third survived to be excavated in 1958 but Orpheus was lost. He had occupied the central octagon within a narrow square frame but the recording obviously misunderstood the figure. Inscription fragments deciphered as 'June' and 'December' suggest that outside the square four seasonal months may have been inscribed. Eight trapezoidal panels contain a series of animals bouncing anticlockwise around the circle. Fragments of a gryphon, a hunting dog, a tigress with prominent teats (together with a 'mirror trap' used to distract by its reflection so that hunters could steal cubs), a leopard, a leaping stag and a boar remained in 1958. As at Horkstow, the animals were backed by trees in the garden sculpture tradition. Beyond this, there is no similarity in the figure work between the two sites and different mosaicists were responsible. An adjoining panel featured a hunting scene of stag and dogs surmounted by a row of four laurel-bordered roundels containing busts of the Seasons.

Newton St Loe's Orpheus mosaic was discovered in 1837 during the construction of the Great Western Railway to Bristol. Most of the seven mosaics found in the villa were carefully recorded, lifted and displayed in Keynsham railway station by Thomas Marsh, a talented young engineer. Alas, thinking this unsuitable, they were afterwards donated to Bristol's early museum. Lacking display space the panels were neglected and presumably stored outside where in a few years they disintegrated into hundreds of pieces. Believed lost, in 1993 ASPROM succeeded in locating them in the Bristol Museum stores where the blackened fragments of all the lifted mosaics were jumbled together in pallets. A small working party led by the author had several weekend sessions cleaning and rough sorting fragments. Following that the author continued the process alone for several years. The operation took place in a store that was in constant use and so pieces had to be returned to pallets after each assembling session. By 2000 sufficient pieces of the Orpheus mosaic had been identified for the author to reassemble it in public on a sand bed in Bristol Museum's entrance hall. Between 85–90 per cent survives and is now stored in sections in Bristol Museum. Fragments from the villa's other pavements were also sorted, boxed and labelled by the author for future reassembly.

The mosaic floored the outer part of a bipartite chamber. The central guilloche-bordered circular panel is occupied by a fine seated Orpheus with his *kithara* and fox. Evidence of prefabrication was noted by the author on this panel and it is notable that the guilloche surrounding Orpheus had to be clumsily raised to accommodate his cap and broken for the fox's tail. Notwithstanding the music, the finely drawn, lively animals in the surrounding circle are not pacified but paired for battle or flight as in the arena. Several fine deciduous and coniferous trees separate them. It is likely that the mosaicists made a mistake in their measurements as one animal and two trees had to be omitted through lack of space. The splendid bear lacks a combatant. This is traditionally a bull but the latter faces a panther. No birds complement the menagerie. The figure work cannot be matched to that of another known mosaic.

Geometric panels surround the mosaic and most survive but lack of space in the sandbox would not allow their display in 2000. A threshold panel linking this mosaic to the

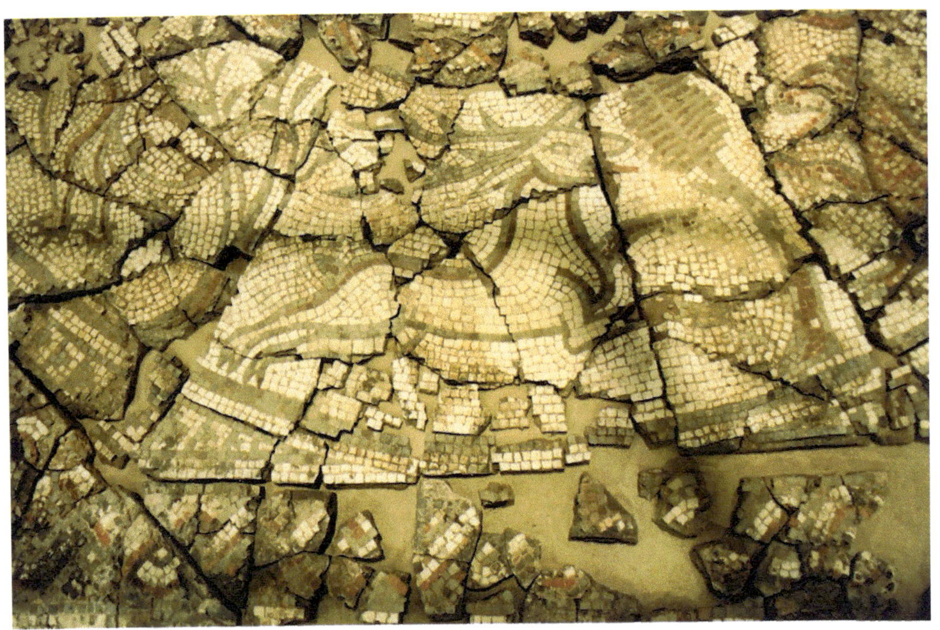

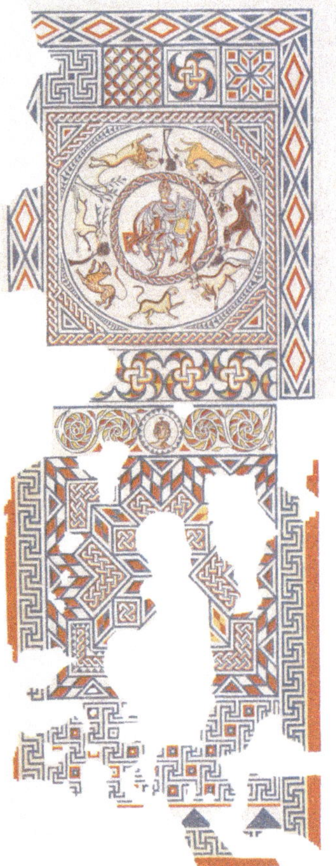

Above: The reassembled Newton St Loe stag and deciduous and evergreen trees. Most of the fragments were black before cleaning started and initial sorting commenced. (Author's photograph)

Left: Stephen Cosh's recording of the complete bipartite chamber holding the Newton St Loe mosaic. The borders of the Orpheus panel survive but it seems likely that only a sample of the damaged inner chamber's mosaic was lifted. (Courtesy and copyright Stephen Cosh)

geometric one of the inner chamber featured a vegetal scroll with a central bust probably of Ceres with a triangular *modius* on her head. Unfortunately this panel is lost and only known from Marsh's recording so its actual appearance is unknown. If the '*modius*' is interpreted as feathers then the bust may be Orpheus' mother, Calliope, the muse of epic poetry and eloquence. What may be her attributes of writing tablets or scrolls rather than a garment appears at her left shoulder. As nothing of the panel survives among the fragments it seems likely that Brunel had it removed to one of the GWR's buildings or directors' houses.

Withington's Orpheus mosaic again featured eight unpacified, joyously bounding animals chasing each other in an anticlockwise procession around the circle surrounding Orpheus and his fox. Attractive trees with lotus-like buds interspersed the animals, segmenting the circle. Narrow panels containing six birds either side of a rosette and two peacocks confronting a central *cantharus* respectively flank the mosaic. At a later date a series of rectangular panels featuring Neptune/Oceanus, marine beasts and running animals were added by the Durnovarian firm. Possibly they were chosen to show Orpheus' dominion over the denizens of the sea as well. The Neptune panel is displayed at the British Museum and five of the animals and the bird panel are in storage there as is the bear in Bristol. This important mosaic could well be restored. Withington's animals and trees cannot be matched to the existing figure work of any other Orpheus mosaicists, although the pose of a cockerel recalls one at Woodchester.

A mosaic excavated at Wellow, Somerset, in 1685 was recorded by the antiquarian John Aubrey. Elaborate geometric borders surrounded a square guilloche frame holding a star of interlaced squares within which was a guilloche-bordered circular panel. Figured fragments within this panel have been identified by the author as misplaced fragments of the *kithara* and garments of Orpheus that bear comparison with those at Littlecote.

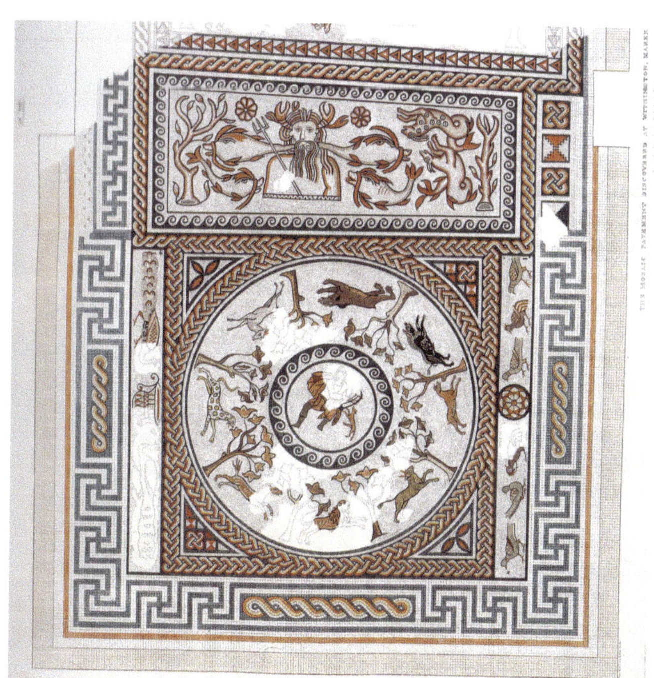

Lysons' recording of the lively but now stored Withington Orpheus and the Neptune panel on display in the British Museum. (Author's collection)

Confronted peacocks and a *cantharus* filled the surviving corner of the square frame. This central square was flanked by side panels holding lost *canthari* between confronted panthers recalling Littlecote's panel. Ivy growing from the *canthari* may echo that at Kemble in the shape of their leaves if Aubrey's drawing can be trusted. Possibly Wellow's mosaicists may have worked at Littlecote and Kemble.

Other Orpheus floors are suspected where historic accounts record mosaics being decorated with 'diverse images of birds and beasts'. Examples include Comb End, Gloucestershire, where birds, fishes and 'circles' were reported and at Caerwent a lion, tiger, stag and parrot were seen. A tantalising glimpse of a possible large Orpheus mosaic was occasioned by metal detectorists Paul Ballinger and John Carter in 2009 at Kemble, near Cirencester. They uncovered part of a well preserved mosaic depicting a possible gryphon. Its right leg is raised. A gently curving border of guilloche suggests that the diameter of the circle is large unless the 'curve' is a badly drawn straight line and the animal is thus within a horizontal panel. A rather crude ivy scroll with distinctive lunette-shaped leaves backs the animal. Unfortunately further professional work at the site did not enlarge the sondage and so more information could not be gleaned.

A lost mosaic with a circular design was found at Pit Meads, Wiltshire, in 1800. It possibly featured a central Orpheus roundel and one circle. An engraving appears to show the legs of a bird in clockwise procession around the circle. In design it possibly resembled the Merida mosaic. High-quality mosaic fragments and indications of a curving design were found at Bishopstone Down, Wiltshire, and hint at an Orpheus mosaic or a hunting scene. Fragments seem to show animal parts such as a hound's head, boar's back, lion's mane and a pheasant tail. Fragments resembling a billowing red *chlamys* might suggest Orpheus.

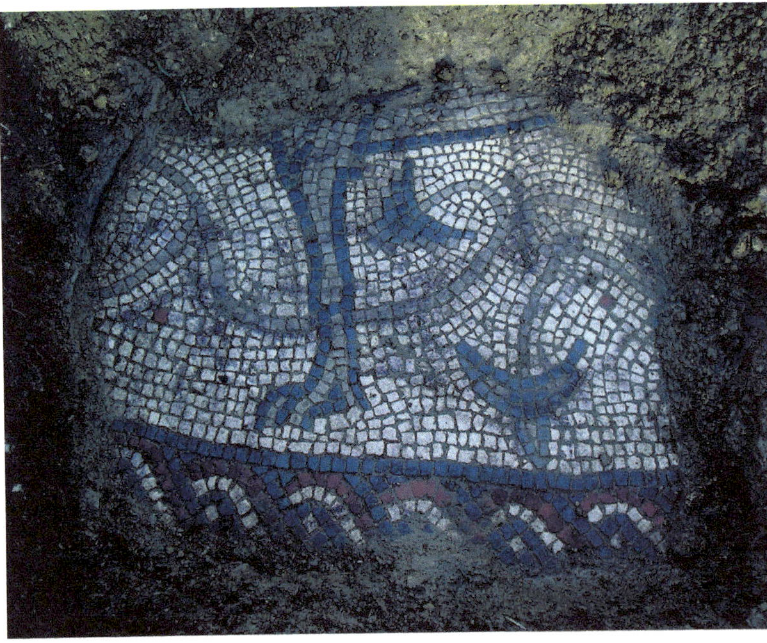

A gryphon or feline from a possible Orpheus mosaic discovered near Kemble, Gloucestershire, in 2009 by Paul Ballinger and John Carter. (Copyright Paul Ballinger)

17

The Boxford Triumphs of Pelops and Bellerophon Mosaic

Excavations in 2017 and 2019 at Mud Hole Villa, Boxford, Berkshire, uncovered an exceptional mosaic flooring a reception room that included two ritual caches of ironwork placed directly opposite each other within its walls. In its design, singular choice of subjects, with their subtle connections linking Neptune/Poseidon, Bellerophon, Pelops, Atlas, horses and the kingdom of Elis, together with an attempt to create a *trompe l'oeil* composition, it sets itself apart from other known Romano-British mosaics and merits special mention here. The sophisticated and interrelated subjects are unmatched in Britain

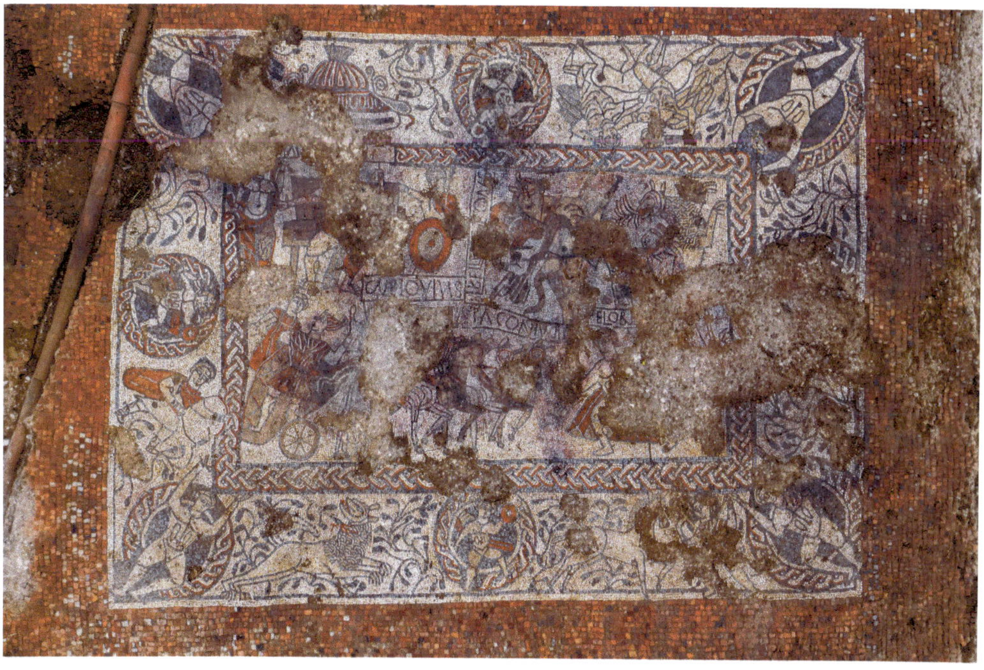

The most important mosaic discovery for over fifty years. The Triumphs of Pelops and Bellerophon mosaic at Boxford, Berkshire. (Copyright David Shepherd)

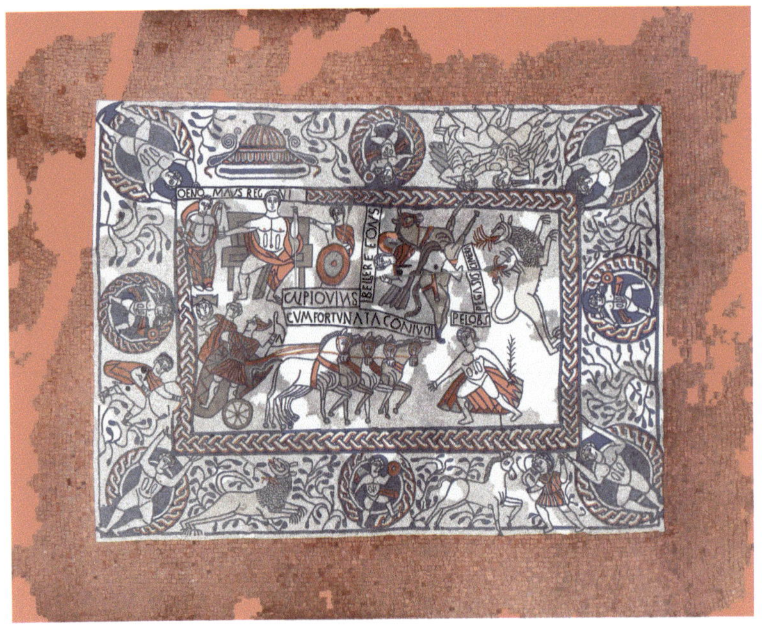

A composite reconstruction of the Boxford mosaic after the author's drawings by Steve Clark. (Copyright Steve Clark after Anthony Beeson on a photograph by Richard Miller)

and in some cases unique. Naive and untidy in its design, the mosaic certainly is, but it possesses great entrancement. Unlike most British figurative pavements its subjects are not confined within panels but flow to each other. Borders are minimal and dispensed with where figure work or inscriptions take precedence. Following a late Roman artistic trend not previously encountered in Britain but commonplace in illumination and ivory work, characters break out of borders. Its Bellerophon panel is Britain's most accomplished, featuring a foreshortened Pegasus. Rare inscriptions and nametags appear, as well as the name of the villa's owner and his wife.

The composition features twenty-eight figures or objects. Its principal subject, the triumph of Pelops over King Oenomaus of Pisa and Elis, only occurs on two mosaics in the entire Roman Empire. One is from Shahba, Syria, and the other monumental version floors a late Roman palace at Noheda, Spain. The subject occasionally decorates sarcophagi in the second and third centuries AD and around eight examples survive. The third-century sarcophagi and later mosaics follow a three-scene artistic formula of depicting the court of Oenomaus followed by the chariot race in which Pelops (Poseidon's ex-cupbearer and lover) won the hand of Princess Hippodamia ('Horse-tamer') and thirdly the united lovers. Had Pelops failed, his head would have joined those of previous suitors hung outside the palace. Oenomaus perished through the bribed treachery of Myrtilus, who substituted a wax linchpin for the metal one in the king's chariot. Boxford's composition is L-shaped. Its court panel features Oenomaus enthroned below a *cantharus* that refers to the meaning of his name 'man of wine'. He displays Hippodamia with his right hand while on his left a palace guard points the viewer to his magnificence. Boxford's guard is the only British representation of an armed man with a shield in contemporary dress. A fragmentary inscription, thought originally by the author to name Hippodamia but tentatively then restored by Dr Roger Tomlin as reading 'OENOMAVS REGNI' ('The Kingdom of

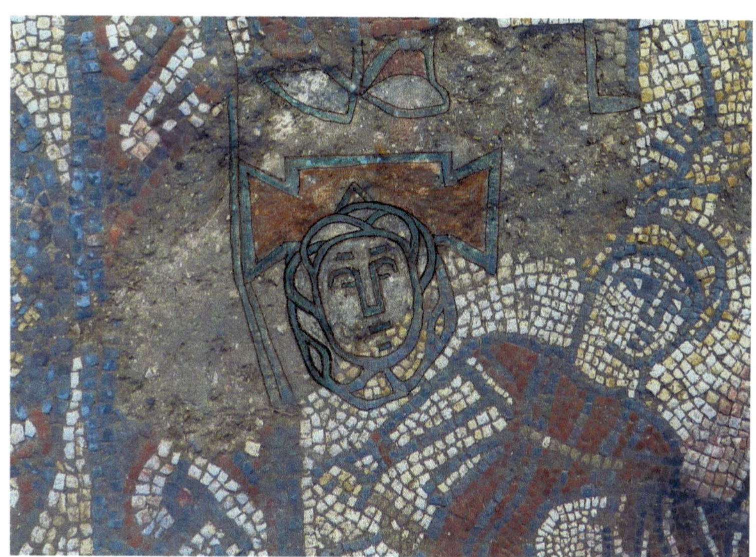

A bearded suitor's head hanging from an ansate board above Myrtilus. Author's reconstruction. (Author's collection)

Oenomaus'), sets the scene. The latter is now thought unlikely by Tomlin and the surviving letters suggest that Hippodamia's name was perhaps followed by a patronymic, or the name of her father in the genitive tense.

Oenomaus is generally bearded but there is no indication here of a beard on the surviving tesserae at his neck. Another interpretation sees the inscription turned outwards and reading 'IN DEO VIVAS' ('May you live in God'), thus putting a Christian element into an otherwise purely pagan design and adapting the *cantharus* into the cup of Christ. This, however, leaves the major character scene (the court of Oenomaus) without any setting or name plate, which would be uncharacteristic judging by the Bellerophon panel, and a story where the hero achieves victory by deceit and two murders seems a strange choice for a Christian mosaic. A severed bearded suitor's head hangs from an ansate panel below Hippodamia. Below this Myrtilus exchanges the linchpin behind his back and faces a charioteer in a stationary racing quadriga. It finishes on the right with Pelops (named 'PELOBS') standing across the finishing line and perhaps once holding a victor's palm branch. The unbearded charioteer is Pelops but was originally assumed to be Oenomaus. He does not wear Pelops' traditional Eastern garb beyond a Phrygian cap and bears no resemblance to the hero's semi-naked named figure. However, characters appear several times in the same composition in ancient narrative art. Boxford's composition is based on an earlier artistic formula than Noheda's and similar to that found on a second-century sarcophagus in Tipasa museum, Algeria. This only depicts Pelops at the palace, the preparations for the race, with the hero and Oenomaus in stationary chariots, and Myrtilus taking a wax pin from its mould. Unlike most depictions the united lovers do not close the scene. Boxford's innovative version merges the court and chariot panels as one in the viewer's mind. Thus, the left side of the mosaic shows Pelops arriving at the palace, viewing the severed head and corrupting Myrtilus, while inside (i.e. above) sits Oenomaus and his court. Knowing the story, the stationary chariot with its chorus line of pawing, impatient horses then suggests the race to the viewer's mind and the figure of Pelops at the finishing line confirms it. Winning and not a romantic ending is the message imparted.

The funerary games given by Pelops for Oenomaus were the mythical origins of the Olympics, and the only known large sculptural group of the myth ornamented the main pediment of Olympia's Temple of Zeus. An inscription, restored by Roger Tomlin, reads 'CAEPIO VIVAS CVM FORTUNATA CONIVGE' ('Long life to you, Caepio, with your wife Fortunata'). Thus Caepio was the villa owner, and the mosaic is possibly a wedding present. A final word may have completed the inscription above the chariot.

The Triumph of Bellerophon (see page 90) filled the space left by the L-shaped Pelops composition. Below its inscription 'BELLEREFONS', the panel would have been the first thing seen by visitors entering from the south and was perhaps used in this context as a flattering comparison to Caepio the local force for good over evil and who set Roman Boxford's world turning. Visitors would be led past this to face the Pelops composition and perhaps the seated Caepio.

The Bellerophon and Pelops panels are loosely contained within the guilloche borders of a 'pergola' upheld at each corner by walking telamones (Atlantes to the Greeks), previously only known on a second-century mosaic from Tusculum, now in the Vatican's Greek Cross Hall. Their presence at Boxford is remarkable and perhaps occasioned by some versions of the story naming the sky-bearing titan Atlas as Pelops' father. Atlas was also the father of Oenomaus' wife Sterope. Uniquely the telamones step from guilloche-bordered blue mandorlas in the manner of Christ in later manuscript paintings such as the sixth-century Rabbula Gospels. They are foreshortened like Hemsworth's Venus, in an attempt to make them appear upstanding. The feet of the south-western telamon and adjacent guilloche of the mandorla are compressed by the coarse border, suggesting the latter was laid first.

In line with the mosaicist's attempts to impart a *trompe l'oeil* dimension to the floor the borders are treated as a bushy landscape wherein heroes triumph. All sides of the border held a central roundel from which an *amorino* burst out holding a crown of triumph, echoing the victories displayed on the floor. They resemble an *amorino* on the Byzantine Veroli casket in the Victoria and Albert Museum, who holds a crown above Bellerophon to honour his bridling of Pegasus. The western *amorino* holds a linchpin in his hand with reference to the chariot panel above. He is the finest, most classical in appearance, and employs tesserae as small as 2 mm across.

In the eastern border Hercules kills a centaur whose legs buckle as he prepares to receive the death blow. He clasps Hercules' wrist while grabbed by the hair. This is the 'fatal pose' the artistic code informing the viewer that those shown using it are doomed. It commonly appears in classical art and the figure of Penthesilea on the Horkstow Medallions Mosaic also adopts it. However, it seems to have been deemed too theatrical for Imperial monuments and is absent from reliefs documenting real campaigns and had mostly died out by the third century. This is one of the latest depictions of this pose known and either depicts Hercules' fight at the cave of Pholus, or a variant killing of Nessus. Hercules was Pelops' descendant and established the pancratium contest at the Olympics in his honour. Beyond the *amorino* the *cantharus* subtly refers to Oenomaus, 'man of wine', in the court panel beyond. Possibly the owner's chair overlooked it.

The southern border only held an *amorino* roundel and bushes, but the northern features an archer identified as Alcathous of Elis, the son of Pelops. Alcathous slew the

Cithaeronian lion and inherited the kingdom of Megara as a result. His daughter Periboea married the hero Telamon, whose name is perhaps another connection to the unrelated telamones.

Alcathous has an importance in the study of British mosaics for he fires an arrow behind the back of the corner telamon to hit a fleeing lion in the western border; thus again attempting a *trompe l'oeil* effect. This combination of incident between borders is unique and something one might expect from a manuscript illumination. The splendid

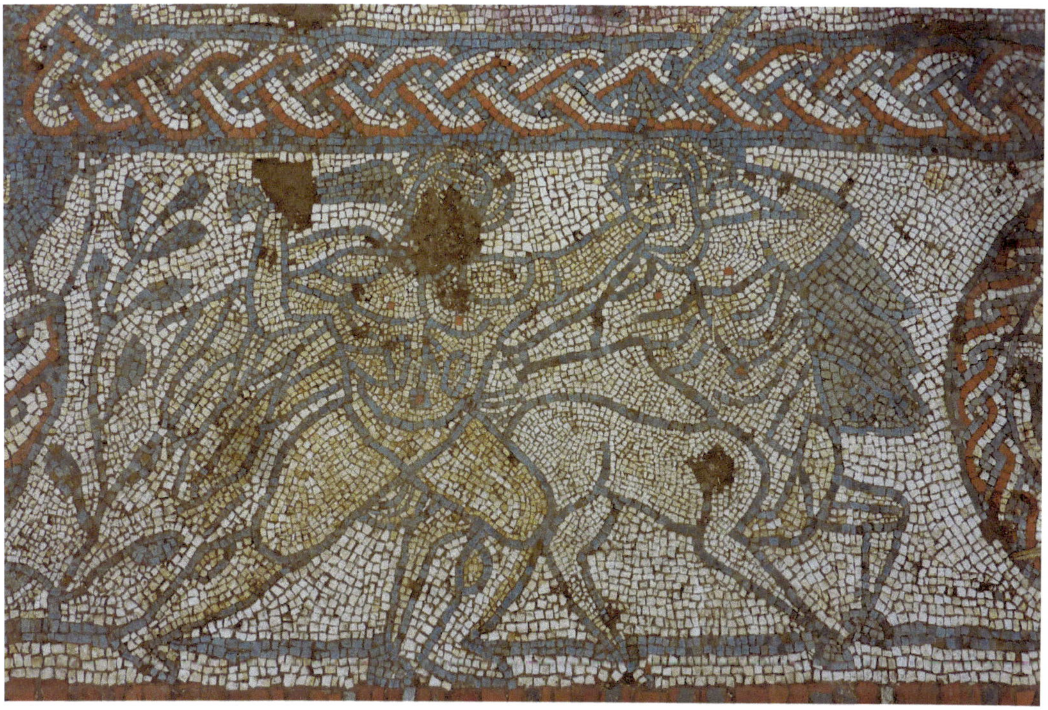

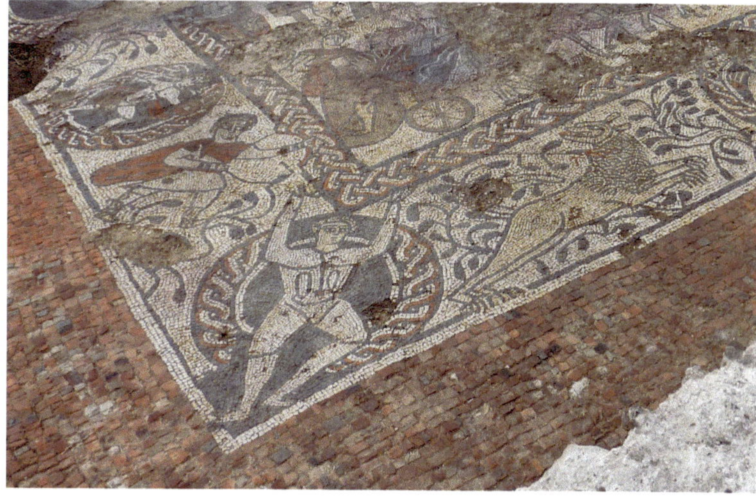

Above: Hercules kills the centaur in the eastern border. (Author's photograph)

Right: Alcathous kills the Cithaeronian lion behind the northern telamon's back. (Author's photograph)

Cithaeronian lion has a red tongue and sharp teeth and was also the model for Chimaera. Alcathous' arrow sticks in his throat and blood spurts forth.

The final subject on the western border features a horse and a finely executed man with a rope or bridle identified as the triumphal taming of Arion by Adrastus of Argos. Arion, like Pegasus, Bellerophon and Chrysaor, was Poseidon's son, this time by Demeter. To avoid his amorous attentions she changed into a mare but he transformed into a stallion and covered her. Arion could both talk and fly and Hercules gave him to Adrastus after his siege of Elis. Adrastus' figure includes some of the smallest tesserae on a British mosaic and yet Arion's is naive compared to the other mounts on the floor and is presumably the work of an apprentice. The group recalls a second-century BC funerary painting from Egnazia called *The Horse Tamer*. Two bas reliefs featured in Johann Winckelmann's *Monumenti antichi inediti*, 1767, depict Arion with his parents Demeter and Poseidon. In one, Pelops stands as cupbearer by Poseidon's couch.

Boxford's mosaicists' innovative approach and attempts to produce a *trompe l'oeil* design is noteworthy. Their mosaic is arguably Britain's most important example of late Roman art. Its importance lies not in the artistic or technical abilities of its mosaicists but in the remarkable and sophisticated choice of subjects depicted, all subtly connected to Pelops, Bellerophon, Poseidon and triumph. All are of great interest and originality in art and must surely have been chosen with care by the patron. It illustrates the cultural awareness of those viewing the pavement, who would be expected to understand and make the connections between the stories depicted. Other British mosaics such as Lullingstone's with its enigmatic inscription, Littlecote's syncretic Orpheus, Horkstow's Medallions Mosaic and Low Ham's Dido and Æneas illustrate the culture and intellectual interests of upper-class Romano-Britons. Although rarely depicted, Pelops' story was related by Socrates, Euripides and others while mythological collections such as Hyginus' *Fabullae* would have provided a treasury of connecting stories. That Pelops' story was chosen for this modest villa, when only two other mosaic representations of the race are known, raises questions as to its patron and origins. How should one account for the spelling of 'Bellerefons' known only from the Malaga mosaic? Is there an Iberian connection either with the mosaic's designer, patron or mosaicist? Comparison with Noheda's mosaic and Pelops sarcophagi show that Boxford's follows an artistic tradition but in its own innovative way. Much of its action takes place in the viewer's mind and there is no actual race depicted. Many of its images such as the unclothed Pelops and Hippodamia, the use of the fatal pose, telamones and its references to the Tipasa sarcophagus, hark back to the second century and yet Bellerophon is clothed and firmly contemporary, as is the imperial imagery of Oenomaus' court. Its lively borders and the naivety of some images recall late Roman manuscript illumination. The eccentricity of figures breaking out of their borders is encountered on fifth-century ivory diptychs that ornamented book covers such as the Bellerophon panel in the British Museum (inventory No. 1856.6-23.2) and on the illuminations themselves. Thus Boxford's mosaicists were actually following a fifth-century fashion found in other artistic media but not yet recognised in British mosaics, suggesting that the mosaic may itself date from that century. Coins of the late fourth and early fifth century were discovered on site. The mosaic may represent a last flowering of the figurative mosaicist's art in Britannia.

Further Reading

Beeson, Anthony, Nichol, Matt, Appleton, Joy, *The Boxford Mosaic: A Unique survivor from the Roman Age* (Countryside Books, 2019)

Cookson, Neil, *Romano-British Mosaics: A Reassessment* (B.A.R, 1984)

Croft, Bob, *Roman Mosaics in Somerset* (Somerset County Council, 2009)

Dunbabin, Katherine, *Mosaics of the Greek and Roman World* (Cambridge University Press, 1999)

Field, Robert, *Geometric Patterns from Roman Mosaics and How to Draw Them* (Tarquin, 1988)

Jesnick, Ilona J., *The Image of Orpheus in Roman Mosaics* (B.A.R, 1997)

Johnson, Peter, *Romano-British Mosaics* (Shire, 1982)

Jones, Christine, *Roman Mosaics* (Museum of London, 1988)

Mackenzie, Caroline K., *Culture and Society at Lullingstone Roman Villa* (Archaeopress, 2019)

Neal, David S., *Roman Mosaics in Britain* (Society for the Promotion of Roman Studies, 1981)

Neal, David S., and Cosh, Stephen R., *Roman Mosaics of Britain*, 4 volumes in 5 (Society of Antiquaries, 2002–10)

Rainey, Anne, *Mosaics in Roman Britain* (David and Charles, 1973)

Rule, Margaret, *Floor Mosaics in Roman Britain* (Macmillan, 1974)

Smith, David J., 'The Mosaic Pavements' in Rivet, A. L. F., *The Roman Villa in Britain* (Routledge, 1969), pp 75–125

Smith, David J., *Roman Mosaics at Hull* (Hull Museums, 2005)

Witts, Patricia, *Mosaics in Roman Britain* (Tempus, 2005)

Witts, Patricia, *A Mosaic Menagerie* (B.A.R., 2016)

New mosaic discoveries in Britain are reported in the membership publications of the popular Association for Roman Archaeology (*ARA and ARA News*), those of ASPROM (*Mosaic* and *Asprom Newsletter*) and the Society for the Promotion of Roman Studies' annual *Britannia.*

Acknowledgements

My grateful thanks to David Ashford, Richard Buckley, Steve Clark, Mark Corney, Stephen Cosh, Robert Field, Chris Forsey, Nich Hogben, Richard Miller, David Neal, David Reeves, David Rider, David Shepherd, Gavin Speed, Luigi Thompson, John Valentin, Bryn Walters and Georgie Webb for the loan of images.

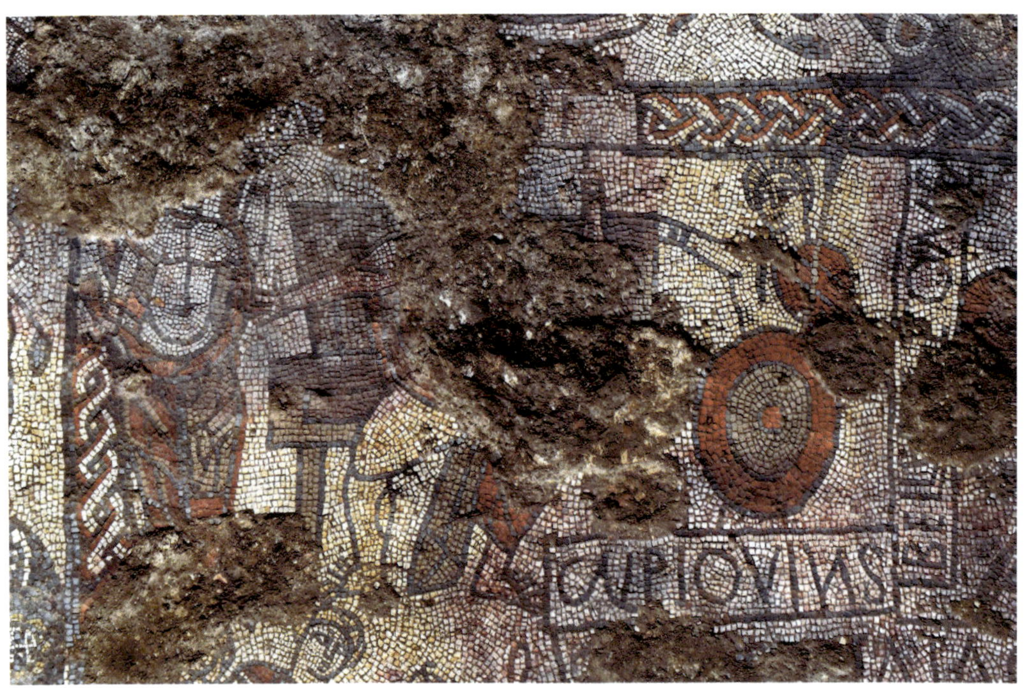

Princess Hippodamia, King Oenomaus and a guard from the Pelops section of the mosaic at Boxford. (Chris Forsey)